Belfast Flashbacks

Stories from Both Sides

Bill Meulemans
Portland State University
The Queen's University of Belfast
Southern Oregon University

While every precaution has been taken in the preparation of this book, the publisher assumes no responsibility for errors or omissions, or for damages resulting from the use of the information contained herein.

BELFAST FLASHBACKS: STORIES FROM BOTH SIDES

First edition. February 7, 2024.

Copyright © 2024 Bill Meulemans.

ISBN: 979-8224897384

Written by Bill Meulemans.

Table of Contents

Books by Bill Meulemans

*The Presidential Majority: Presidential Campaigning
in Congressional Elections* (1970)

Making Political Choices: An Introduction to Politics. (1989)
Belfast: Both Sides Now. (2013)
How the Left and Right Think: The Roots of Division
In American Politics (2019)

*Dynamiting the Siskiyou Pass and Other Short Stories
From Oregon and Beyond.* (2023)

Belfast Flashbacks: Stories From Both Sides. (2024)

Website: **billmeulemans.com**

Preface

When I first arrived in Northern Ireland, I was prepared to stay a few weeks with the hope of gaining a personal understanding of why this conflict had continued on for hundreds of years. I had just come from Israel, and I had an interest in comparing the two long-standing disputes. My primary focus was to see how an average person could adapt to a life in a conflict that had raged on for as long as anyone could remember.

But after a short time in Belfast, I began to see things from a different perspective. It wasn't long before I became fascinated with the many sides of life in the North of Ireland. I developed close friendships with people who lived less than a mile apart, but whose lives would never touch. And secondly, I was amazed by the hospitality of the people on both sides of the conflict. Belfast became my home away from home.

The result was that I made 21 trips from Portland, Oregon to Northern Ireland over a 14-year period. A teaching position at The Queen's University of Belfast for 11 years gave me a compensation package that made it possible for me to return again and again. My daily on-the-ground research became a way of life for me. I never tired of my time in all the small neighborhoods and towns around the North. I knew all the nooks and crannies of Belfast better than I knew my own home town in the US.

As time went on, however, I began to wonder why my commitment to live and work in Belfast was so compelling. There was a mysterious personal connection to Ireland, especially to Belfast. I spent many hours reading old Irish newspapers that dated back to the nineteenth century. I can't say I have memories of a past era, but I do have unique personal historical insights that I can't explain.

Strangely, I can empathize with both communities on a personal level. It is as though I've had the experience of living lives before on rival sides of the city. There is no difficulty for me in seeing the conflict through the eyes of both working-class Catholics and Protestants. For me the conflict is personal. It's hard to explain, but I've always felt an unusual commitment to both sides.

This book, *Belfast Flashbacks,* was motivated by forces that I do not completely understand.

1. Opening Doors

My first arrival in Northern Ireland was memorable. I was in the middle of the Irish Sea on a ferryboat crossing over from Scotland. There was an announcement on the boat that I was to report to the customs officials in a particular compartment on the ferry. My name was mispronounced, but there was no question that someone on board wanted to talk with me.

Soon I was ushered into a small room with three official-looking guys in two-tone blue uniforms. It was clear from the beginning that they had some doubts about why I was going to Ulster. Before I could sit down, they started asking questions in rapid order:

> "Who are you really?"
> "Where did you come from?"
> "Why are you going to Northern Ireland?"
> "Who do you know there?"
> "Why were you in Israel?"
> "Do you have any contacts in the PLO or the IRA?"

I was cramped into a small compartment with three men with British accents peppering me with questions. The year before, I had been in the Middle East where political violence was rampant, so my passport entries must have set off alarm bells. The customs officials seemed convinced that I was coming to their country to stir up trouble. Out of the blue one of them shouted, "Where did you get that suntan? Did you just come from the Middle East?" Another one added, "With our weather here, no one in Northern Ireland ever comes by a suntan honestly." They obviously thought I was a gunrunner bringing weapons from the PLO into Ireland. The one holding my passport said, "We're going to keep our eye on you."

As they blew cigarette smoke in my face, I answered the questions the same way, over and over again:

> "My name is Bill Meulemans. I'm an American professor of political science."

"I'm going to Northern Ireland to do research on the conflict."

"I don't know anyone in Ulster."

"I was in Israel on a Fulbright scholarship."

"I don't know anyone in the PLO or the IRA."

I suppose I could have been offended, but their concern about strangers bringing in illegal weapons was justified. Thousands were killed by guns from the outside, and some of the arms and explosives had come from the Middle East. As I came to understand later, tracking down the weapons of war would probably be the easy part of ending this conflict. The hard part would be healing the agonizing communal memories of more than 800 years of division. The toll of this war went far beyond the body counts. The dead have all been buried, but the survivors still carry an aching bitterness in their hearts. It will not disappear soon, if ever. You could still feel it in the air. On some days, you could cut it with a knife.

At first, I thought it was just my imagination, but when I first arrived in Belfast, I had a feeling that sent chills down my spine. At the beginning, I attributed my apprehensions to the armed troops on the street, the sand bags around the security checkpoints, and the plastic shopping sacks blowing in the breeze from the barbed-wire fences. I certainly was afraid because of the internal war around me, but this feeling was different than any personal fears that I could understand.

Later, I realized that there was an unmistakable sense of *evil* hanging in the air, and that it was the product of all the brutality of an eternal conflict that had gone on for hundreds of years. I soon realized that *Belfast and its environs were haunted* – that there were thousands of lost souls present who had died tragically in a war that had gone on for hundreds of years.

But my gut reaction to Belfast was not new to me. It was the same ominous feeling I had when I was in other haunted places. It was there when I interviewed Klan members in Mississippi and Louisiana. I also felt it when I entered the refugee camps on the West Bank in Israel. After years of thinking about it, I have come to the conclusion that, in all those places, what I actually felt was the raw emotion of human hatred. It was like a heavy fog that settled over the land, something that will probably linger on for many generations. After a while, I wondered if I was the only one who could feel it?

Several months later, I began bringing up this topic with close friends from both communities. Many (but not all) said they felt it some of the time, but they experienced it most keenly whenever they returned from a trip to the South and crossed the border coming back into the North. Even on a train at night (where there were no visible physical border signs) some of my friends could feel the negative emotions when crossing over into the North. It was like passing from one side of an invisible curtain to the other. The change in atmosphere made one shudder.

But I did find a few places where the "fog of Belfast" – as I called it – had been swept away, at least temporarily. My first sense of relief came the first week as I walked past the Europa Hotel on a Tuesday evening in downtown Belfast. From out in the street, I could hear the unmistakable sound of a modern jazz band. I went inside and soon came to know all the members of a home-grown jazz quartet. Every Tuesday evening and Saturday afternoon, I hung out at the Europa with folks that played *my* kind of music. During all my 14 years in Belfast, jazz was my escape. The musicians from both religions became my close friends. We talked about jazz, not the Troubles.

The jazz venue at the Europa became my emotionally "safe place" in Belfast. Sometimes I just wanted to get away from all that was happening out on the street. In some ways it was my sanctuary until I found out that the Europa Hotel had been bombed more times than any other hotel in Western Europe (33 times between 1972 and 1992). But I always went back on Tuesday evenings and Saturday afternoons because, as I told my friends, the music was good for my soul.

Another refuge I found was in the political science department at The Queen's University of Belfast. Here was an opportunity for me to become acquainted with fellow university faculty members who would also be informed sources on the conflict. The first faculty member I got to know was Professor Cornelius O'Leary who taught the "Politics of the USA" course. From the beginning we filled a void for each other. We thoroughly enjoyed each other's company.

"Con," as he was called, loved to talk about American politics, and I wanted to know more about the North of Ireland. Our friendship blossomed into a mutual arrangement whereby Con introduced me to anyone and everyone he knew in Ireland – both North and South – and we discussed all the interesting scandals in American politics.

Within a few days, Con asked me to come to his class as a guest lecturer in his course. Later he introduced me to all his colleagues in the Politics Department at The Queen's University of Belfast. It was an association that would last for all my years in Belfast. It was my home base where I could always get a factual account of Irish history across the entire island.

It wasn't long before Con asked me to do several lectures because his health was failing. I took over his course for the last eight weeks of the semester, and I soon became a quasi-official member of the faculty. My experience was that Irish students were "starved" to learn more about the United States. They asked me many informed questions about American politics, and I in turn, heard their personal stories about Northern Ireland. My Irish students and I developed a mutually affirming relationship.

After I had taught the "Politics of the USA" class for several weeks, I decided to do a student evaluation of the course which turned out rather well. I put the evaluation results on the desk of the department chair, and after consulting with the other department members, the head of the department offered me a position to teach the "Politics of the USA" course the next year. As it turned out, Con was retiring and I would continue teaching the class for the next 11 years. I was really fortunate to get this position. I soon became a visiting professor and unofficial member of the Politics Department at The Queen's University of Belfast, one of the premier universities in Ireland with a world-class reputation.

My position on the Queen's faculty gave me a certain legitimacy on the street. I had some business cards printed that highlighted my association with the local institution of higher education that was respected all over the United Kingdom and Ireland. I was told many times that few, if any, of the university faculty ever came into the working-class neighborhoods of Belfast. Those business cards opened many doors for me. I handed out hundreds of them during my time in Ulster.

I had a very productive interaction with the university, but I wanted the freedom to move about Ulster. So, I had all my university responsibilities scheduled for Mondays and Tuesdays of each week, so I had the other five days free. When I wasn't in the classroom on those two days, I was out on the street in both the Catholic and Protestant working-class neighborhoods of Belfast and other towns in the North. During those early years, I learned a lot more about underlying issues from local folks than I did from the university faculty.

My contacts in Ireland ranged from well-known elected officials and the clergy, to not so well-known paramilitary members, and nearly everyone in between. I found them to be some of the warmest people I had ever known. It was a surprise to me, but after a few years, the northern Irish welcomed me into their churches, homes, and pubs. It was beginning to feel like home.

At first, I believed the safest place in Belfast was on the grounds of the university, thinking that certainly the campus was immune from the conflict, but I was wrong. A student was shot and killed not far from my classroom. There were no places where an individual could truly feel safe. A person could be targeted in their private home, inside a crowd at a sporting event, or even in an open field out in a rural area. The sectarian battlefield was everywhere in the six counties of Northern Ireland. There were many innocent people killed that just happened to be in the wrong place at the wrong time. Everyone had to factor that in as they went about their daily routine.

Because of the widespread nature of the conflict, I felt like I was doing research everywhere I went. I could sense the anxiety among folks in a grocery store, standing in line at a bus stop, or having a cup of coffee in a small cafe. Everyone else must have felt it too, but the northern Irish are not easily intimidated. With few exceptions they refused to stay at home behind locked doors. Every day they went to work and met with friends in their neighborhood pubs.

Some of my most important research was done in drinking clubs in the working-class part of towns throughout the North. I always felt I was "working" even when I was sharing a pint with a new friend. But I must have stood out in these neighborhood haunts because I was the guy with the American accent with an endless number of questions. But the northern Irish of both communities put up with me on a daily basis. After a short time, they could sense that I meant no harm to anyone.

My best friends in Belfast were folks from opposing sides who knew what it was like to live under a daily threat. They had an endless number of tales. Most of them reflected how the conflict had changed their lives. I recall a married couple who told me of their first date. The young woman was wearing a new white dress. She spent days planning for that date and she was all dressed up to go out with her new friend. But on the way home, she and her young man were forced to crawl under a car for cover from a local gunfight in their neighborhood. She remembers that evening as the beginning of a wonderful love relationship, but it also completely ruined her brand-new white dress. I found there was an endless supply of stories that reflected what life was like living in the middle of a sectarian conflict.

There were so many complicated factors in life. For example, some of my most trusted friends had served time in prison. But being a convicted felon in Belfast was different than it was in any other part of the world. If it had not been for the conflict, these men and women would have never seen the inside of a jail cell. Going to prison was actually a badge of honor for many of them, and it deserved respect in some circles. Sometimes, it was the man that had not been in prison that stood out. I recall one guy who always had to explain *why he had never been arrested.*

Former Catholic prisoners even had their own bar in West Belfast called the "Felon's Club." When I first came to Belfast, I tried to enter that establishment by myself, but I was turned away by a husky doorkeeper. The big guy came around from behind the bar and said, "You didn't really mean to come in here, did you?" It was the most compassionate way I have ever been kicked out of a bar. But later – in the company of others – I was able to drop by for a pint without any trouble. After a while, the big guy actually became a friend of mine.

As I look back, I can see that I was carefully being "let inside" of the world of those who were doing the fighting and dying. After several years, there was a time in both communities when I was invited to "functions" or "events" in private homes where nearly everyone present had either served time in prison or had been fortunate to escape the authorities. The relaxed atmosphere in those settings was the sign that people could talk freely without fear that it would be repeated outside the room. I saw this as an indication of trust that I would never betray.

According to my close friends, this process of being "let inside" was very unusual in my case because I made certain that everyone knew I had close friends on the other side. Because of this, there were times when a conversation was a bit strained as more sensitive issues were discussed.

A major part of my neutrality in the North was based on the fact that I was not Irish, Scottish, or English. My own ancestral heritage is a mixture of Belgian, German, and Swiss, which put me in another category safely outside the major nationalities in the conflict. The name "Meulemans" was new to nearly everyone. If my name would have been O'Brien or Stewart, I wouldn't have been able to move around so easily inside of Ulster. I always told my friends, "My body was Belgian, but my heart was northern Irish of both religious traditions. Not being on either side was a critical part of my public identity.

Neutrality was always on my mind. For my own sense of personal honesty, I had to avoid taking sides. Whenever I felt even a faint sense of favoritism for one side in the conflict, I would intentionally reach out to the other side to focus more on their particular situation. In order to do my research, I felt the need to walk the thin line between the two communities. My personal motto had two important parts: "Always look at the other side of an issue, and never tell a lie." No matter what happened I had to be true to myself and the folks I called my friends. Yet, after a few months, that feeling of being in the "middle" became more comfortable, but I was still pretty much alone as a "neutral" in Belfast. There were few if any persons who were truly unbiased.

I had one middle-class friend who was very kind and thoughtful about everyone he mentioned. I made the mistake of assuming that such a person was the exception to the rule, he couldn't be such a thoroughly nice guy and still harbor sectarian attitudes. Then one day, he began to tell me about some people he knew on the other side of town. All of a sudden, I could see that this man was just as sectarian as other folks I knew. He was just better at hiding it.

One of my best friends used to tease me about my "neutrality image." He would tell me terrible stories about the other side and then ask, "How can you overlook that? How can you avoid taking sides?" I would always smile and say, "Well someone has to stand in the middle or there will never be any chance for peace."

This matter of neutrality was not only important for political reasons, it was foundational for me on a psychological level. When I felt tension or uncertainty in a new situation, I would tell myself that my motives were not partisan, that I truly didn't side with either the Catholics or the Protestants. It was this kind of self-talk that enabled me to go into areas that might have been unsafe for others. It was absolutely necessary for me to feel objective, or I might have found myself taking sides in the conflict. It was absolutely important for me to "stand in the middle."

I believe that non-verbal communication is a powerful force, and that many folks can "read" a situation by tuning into how people "feel" who are nearby. I'm not sure that my thoughts on this subject were shared by many others, but I do know it worked for me. I believe that my internal honesty was my greatest asset, and I think it was felt by other people I had contact with throughout the province.

2. Listening and Learning

My routine in Belfast was set by a commitment to never stop working and never stop listening. I started my day on Monday and Tuesday mornings with tutorials at Queen's University. On those two days, I had personal contact each day with two sets of 15 students where we discussed American politics. That was a total of 60 new students each year during a period of 11 years. The students at Queen's University were the brightest, most inquisitive young people I have ever encountered. They were "the cream of the crop" in the North, and they were hungry to learn.

I was fortunate to have a turnover of several hundred young students in my large lecture section each year. In addition, I had evening sessions with adult students that gave me a different reaction on current events in Ireland. I discovered the adult students were equally inspired to learn about politics. An unexpected pleasure was that my evening classes often ended with a follow-up gathering in a local pub. My education on Irish politics continued on many different levels.

Nearly all of my students were graduates of Northern Ireland secondary schools that were identified with either the Protestant or Catholic faith. Coming to Queen's was (for most of them) their first chance to be in the same room with someone from the "other side." At first, I assumed students filled my lecture hall with no particular order, but later I found that the Catholics sat on the left side and the Protestants filled the chairs on the right. In one of my classrooms, there were two doors. After the first few class meetings, I noticed that my students voluntarily "segregated" themselves through the doorways as well. My students had practiced this art of separation all their lives, and it continued in their university education.

Contacts with individual students were an important part of my learning process. It was my first opportunity to meet young people from both communities. I found that many of them (not all) wanted to promote real peace in Northern Ireland. Many students sought me out in my little office on campus to tell me truly terrible things that had happened in their families. They spoke of "thugs" who tried to break into their homes in the early morning hours. Sometimes the intruders were paramilitary members, other times they were the police. These students were only 18 years old, but they already had trouble sleeping at night.

On Wednesdays through Sundays, however, I was out in the field all day, rain or shine. Sundays were my worst day because the Protestant establishment had shut down nearly all activity centers, including most pubs. The city authorities even chained up the swings in the playgrounds because they thought children should be in church or at home. I learned early that the ruling Protestant elites were a pretty grumpy bunch. It didn't appear that they wanted anyone else to enjoy themselves. These church leaders were a pretty thin-lipped crowd. They didn't smile very often.

Many of my free mornings were spent with my friends who drove black taxis in the largest Catholic and Protestant districts of West Belfast. Taxi drivers on the Falls Road carried passengers into the largest Irish Catholic neighborhoods in the North. These drivers had an association with the Irish Republican Army (IRA). I also had friends who drove taxis on the Shankill Road which fed into the largest working-class Protestant areas in West Belfast. These drivers were all linked with the Ulster Volunteer Force (UVF).

My combined time with these taxi drivers gave me a personalized view of the Troubles from the vantage point of people who were "involved" on the street level. There was no question, taxi drivers were my most reliable source of information in the whole province. They had spent their entire lives on the sharp edges of the conflict. I cherished my friendships with them.

In addition, I regularly visited friends in the prison that housed prisoners from both sides. Protestants called the prison by the official name, "The Maze," because it was located in the Maze townland. Catholics called it "Long Kesh" or "The Kesh" because it was located on an old Royal Air Force base by that name. One of the quickest ways of determining the religious membership of a person was to ask someone what they called the prison? That approach never failed me.

I was surprised to note how the Catholic and Protestant paramilitary organizations had drawn up workable rules governing prison visits. Inside the prison, individual inmates (who had tried to kill each other on the outside) could peacefully meet their friends and families in a small visiting room, just a few feet apart.

As these well-known men moved around the room, I heard them mumble to each other, "excuse me" or "pardon me." It was amazing how well these convicted paramilitary members could *get along* inside the neutral ground of the prison meeting room. Everyone seemed to know the "rules" of the game.

After a few years in the North, I came around to understand that the level of sectarian hatred was much higher among some folks who went to church every Sunday, than it was with men who were serving time in prison. There was a certain amount of chivalry between paramilitary members that was completely absent among those who stayed at home reading their Bibles. *I heard more justifications for violence in some of the churches around the province than from the men on both sides serving time in prison.* Long conversations with paramilitary members (on both sides) were an important learning experience for me.

Sectarianism could be put aside (for personal reasons) by these prisoners during visiting hours. Prison guards were in the visiting area, but there was an unwritten understanding that they stayed at one end of the room, often turning their heads away, and ignoring what was going on. There was actually some privacy in the small meeting booths. Most visitors and prisoners had the good sense to turn away when prisoners and their partners were having intimate moments. I have heard from several sources that wives and girlfriends became pregnant in the open room while visiting the prison.

But there were still undercurrents of tension in the prison. When I was with loyalists' visitors, I noticed a certain "independence" as they interacted with prison officials. At the end of the visiting period, prison guards (or warders as they were called) informed everyone it was time to leave. The loyalist prisoners I was visiting would ignore the announcement and as he did a "stare down" with the guard as a means of showing some measure of defiance. In my experience, republican prisoners did not have that same association with the guards. The prison guards and the Irish Republican Army (IRA) were never on good terms. I never saw a trace of communication between them.

Northern Ireland had to be one of the few places in the world where prisoners were given a pass to go home for major holidays. The understanding was that the program would be cancelled if anyone did not return at the scheduled time. Unlike prisoners in other countries, there was a cohesive quality among paramilitary members. They might have been guilty of murder and mayhem, but there was a high degree of trust within their illegal organizations, and to some extent, with the paramilitary groups on the other side.

The northern Irish authorities also had what they called "ordinary decent criminals" (ODC). These were those *not* associated with any paramilitary groups. They included persons convicted of illegal activities such as burglaries selling drugs, and nonpolitical street crime. This term was used most of all by the police and the British government, who put them a special category because these criminals were not guilty of "terrorism." Nearly everyone looked down on ODC prisoners, but they had a certain distinction in society. Only in Northern Ireland would drug dealers and street robbers ever be considered "decent."

At home in Oregon and California, I visited high-security American prisons and found them to be very different from those in Northern Ireland. By comparison, US prisons are a very tough place, very regimented, where everyone is on guard all the time. In the North, however, paramilitaries on both sides considered themselves to be prisoners of war (POWs). Compared to American prisons, there was a semi-relaxed atmosphere inside Irish prisons.

But there was a real difference in how the prison warders treated members of the two opposing communities. Prison staff members were usually Protestants who lived in the same neighborhoods as loyalist prisoners, and it was said the warders felt the pressure from outside the prison to give "favorable treatment" to their fellow Protestants. I knew one warder whose wife had opened a letter bomb that was meant for him. His wife's face was so disfigured that she seldom left her home after that incident. Another prison guard told me he had to move his family several times because he feared being held responsible for actions he had taken inside the prison. It soon became apparent to me that the conflict extended into every part of northern Irish society.

When I was with republican prison visitors from the Catholic side, I was searched very carefully. But when going through with Protestants, there was more of a relaxed atmosphere. Repeatedly I watched Protestant loyalists' visitors passing computer discs that were probably filled with important information. One prisoner I knew quite well actually wrote a column for a newspaper printed outside the prison. It was clear that the prison guards were playing favorites with the visitors.

The prison was generally a serious place, but there were stories there that made everyone smile. I heard a well-known tale about an IRA prisoner who had always helped his elderly father dig up the soil in the garden before spring planting. One year, the son couldn't help with the garden because he was in prison. Knowing full well that all his out-going letters were read by a prison censor, he wrote to this father, "Whatever you do, don't dig in the garden. That's where I buried all the guns." The next morning, 15 husky British soldiers showed up at his father's house and dug up the entire garden and prepared it for spring planting.

Stories where the "Brits" were the object of ridicule were told with glee on both sides of town. Both the republicans and loyalists delighted in pointing out that the British were so self-centered that they often overlooked obviously good ideas in Ireland. While the British came up with all sorts of sophisticated, expensive programs designed to bring both sides together, the programs often failed. I knew a small group of community workers from both sides who came up with a plan that cost very little, but actually worked very well.

Citizen groups on both sides, raised money to provide free mobile cell phones to people in selected neighborhoods who served as an early warning system to report unexpected incursions or hostile activities in areas where people felt insecure. It was a sensible idea that included folks from all over Belfast, and most of all, it served to de-escalate tensions along the walls between working-class neighborhoods.

Some other Belfast people came up with a multitude of creative ideas to break down sectarian boundaries. I developed a friendship with a progressive Presbyterian minister, Bill Shaw, who specialized in ways to de-escalate the conflict. He recognized that there were a lot of Catholic and Protestant boxing fans in Belfast. With this in mind, he built a boxing ring in his church buildings to attract "fighters" and fans from both sides. He also sponsored Alcoholics Anonymous meetings and he brought in volunteers to help parents with autistic children. Bill Shaw's approach was to come in as a "non-sectarian outsider" who could be trusted because he came up with common-sense solutions to real problems. He had a pragmatic approach that bypassed all the old sectarian obstacles of working together across the divide. He has been recognized for his work on both sides.

In a related area, I found out that Belfast people are often willing to trust someone who comes in from the outside. An example of this came up one evening as I voiced an opinion on the weather to a young man standing beside me in the Crown Bar across the street from the Europa Hotel. We soon began to chat and he told me he was a British soldier (not in uniform) based in England, but on home-leave in Belfast to visit his family. Within minutes he was answering my questions about the inherent problems of the British Army operating in the North, and how he felt when he was stationed in Belfast and went out on patrol in Catholic neighborhoods. After fifteen minutes of intense conversation, another man moved up to the bar beside us, and the dialogue ended abruptly. Later, after the new man wandered away, we resumed our friendly exchange. In hushed tones the off-duty soldier said, "You can't be too careful about strangers!"

Yet the northern Irish seem to tell their personal accounts of tragedy more quickly to strangers like myself. One day I was riding a city bus and struck up a conversation with a woman in her late 30s from the Catholic housing estate of Twinbrook in West Belfast. She recounted a time when she lived in a mixed neighborhood where her seven-year-old Catholic son had Protestant playmates. She said the playmates tried to carve the initials "UVF" (Ulster Volunteer Force) on the leg of her son, and later, as she dried his tears, he asked if he could become a Protestant. "I'm sure mommy," he said, "my mates would treat me better if I were a Protestant."

Visitors to Northern Ireland are told many stories of this kind that highlight the barbaric nature of the conflict. Today, however, tourists ride around on double-decker tour buses, snapping pictures of places where (the tour guide tells them) a particular number of people were killed by a bomb, but when they return home, they will have forgotten how many died at each location and whether they were Catholics or Protestants.

But the local people will remember. They remember everything.

3. He Kicks with the Wrong Foot

Usually, I could follow along in a conversation with anyone in Belfast, but one day I heard something that just didn't make sense. A group of taxi drivers were talking about someone I didn't know and one of them added the comment: "You know, he kicks with the wrong foot." I noticed the other guys nodded, indicating they understood about someone who "kicked with the wrong foot." I didn't ask directly what was meant, but I listened more carefully and it finally surfaced that the person in question was a member of the other religious community.

Later I asked several people what it really meant to them? They usually hesitated and they then stammered something like. "That's hard to say. It means they are not tuned into our way of life." Others added that it meant, "They are different from us. They'll never understand us or be accepted by us." The emphasis was that these people are "separate" from us, that they are in "opposition" to us; "There's no way we can ever live in peace with them."

It turned out that I knew a lot of folks "who kicked with the wrong foot." It was just a simple way of saying that they're "not like us," and in some cases, they don't deserve the same respect or compassionate treatment as "our people."

I was to witness an extreme example of this one evening when I visited a Catholic family that lived outside of Belfast. Their daughter was in my political science classes at Queen's University and she wanted me to meet her parents, who had some friends in Oregon. It happened that I came to visit on an evening when the family was going through a real crisis. Their teen-age son had a motorcycle, and on that particular day, he went riding on the Shankill Road, which goes through the largest Protestant working-class neighborhood in Belfast. In retrospect, it was a foolish thing to do. He should have known that it was a dangerous for him to be in the wrong part of town.

The young man was going too fast as he went around a corner and he lost control and crashed in the middle of the street. It wasn't a fatal accident, but the boy was hurt, and trapped under his own motorcycle. A group of young local guys were first on the scene after the accident. The first question from the local gang was, "Are you a Catholic or a Protestant? The boy lied on the assumption that he could masquerade as a Protestant. But the gang of boys followed it up with another question, "Can you sing the Sash My Father Wore?" It's a song that nearly every Protestant knows. But when the young Catholic couldn't sing the song, the other boys began to kick him in the head. A police officer rescued the boy and took him to the hospital for treatment.

Later, his parents picked him up at the hospital. He had been diagnosed as having a severe concussion from the kicking he received while trapped under his motorcycle. That evening all the family could talk about was how their son was beaten up just because he didn't know the words to a sectarian song. He was attacked by a gang just because he was a Catholic. But in the vernacular of West Belfast, "He kicked with the wrong foot."

For many people like that teen-aged boy, religious identity is like race. A person is born as either Catholic or Protestant, and there's not much they can do about it. For most young working-class people, it decides not only their religious membership, but nearly everything else in life as well. It determines what part of town they live in, their political attitudes, the school they attend, their friendships, who they date and marry, where they are buried when they die, and most of all, their personal identity in a sectarian tribe. To my surprise, some Belfast folks can't seem to break free of this kind of thinking, even when they travel abroad.

I was reminded of this everlasting factor when a Protestant married couple from Belfast came to visit me in the United States. They arrived late one evening and the next morning I took them on a walking tour of my neighborhood in Aurora, Oregon. After surveying the homes on my street, the husband asked me how many of my neighbors were Protestants and how many were Catholics? I was completely surprised by the question because I had never thought about my neighbors' religious affiliation, and I really didn't care.

Later that same day, I was driving that Belfast couple around downtown Portland, Oregon where we saw two uniformed police officers walking down the street. The husband wanted to know if the police generally favored Catholics or Protestants. Again, I was surprised. I said American police officers have been criticized for many things, but to my knowledge, it has never been a matter of favoring a particular religious group.

The whole discussion about neighbors and police officers caused me to think more deeply about religious identity in Belfast. I started thinking that religious membership in Northern Ireland is more about culture and politics than it is about theology. I never knew anyone in Belfast who was out trying to convert folks from one side to the other. Most of the people I knew didn't go to church on a regular basis. A lot of them didn't believe in God, but they were all living out their lives securely within their religious identity.

Before I came to Northern Ireland, I wondered if the northern Irish would want to know about *my* religious membership. Maybe they would want to know whether "I kicked with the wrong foot." Surprisingly, very few people seemed to care which church I attended. I think they first noticed my American accent, which caused them to view me as an outsider in their eyes. But there were a few folks that still wanted to know about my religious preference.

While in Belfast, I always made it a practice to attend a different Protestant or Catholic church every Sunday morning or evening. I never stopped learning about folks who lived in embattled neighborhoods. On one occasion, I attended a religious meeting in a small store-front church on the Protestant Shankill Road. After the service, the parishioners asked if I wanted to join them for tea or coffee. They were very generous as they offered me biscuits (what we would call cookies in the US). There were about ten church-goers that gathered around me asking why I was in Belfast. Being on the faculty at Queen's University satisfied nearly everyone, but one older gentleman could not help himself: he really wanted to know whether I was a Protestant or a Catholic.

His first comment was, "Tell me something about yourself?" I knew what he wanted to know, but I chose to ignore the real meaning of his question. I told him I grew up in a small town in northwestern Wisconsin. He shook his head and said, "No, I want to know about your family." By this time, I was having fun. I replied that I had one brother and three sisters. At this point he was getting frustrated and he just blurted out, "How would people identify you back home?" I smiled and said, "All my friends know I am a liberal Democrat." The older man just shook his head and walked away.

There were other times I thought people must have wondered more seriously about my religious background, but the question seldom surfaced when I was interviewing people. There was one time, however, when it did come up under rather trying circumstances. I was inside the Rathcoole Club, a loyalist drinking pub in North Belfast, with two well-known leaders of the Ulster Defense Association (UDA). One of them had a reputation of being a violent man who sometimes lost his temper and killed people on the spot. I had never met that first man before, but I did know the other man rather well.

Just before I met with them, there were reports that the first man had mistakenly killed a young woman who was mentally disadvantaged. The word on the street was that he had shot and killed her because he thought she was a Catholic. Her body was found in a dumpster near some abandoned buildings in North Belfast. Other members of the UDA were angry, not because he had killed someone, but because he had killed *one of his own.*

Unlike other interviews sessions, this one was a bit tense from the very beginning. The man with the violent reputation asked me a lot of questions as to why I was in Belfast and what I thought about certain disagreements with the UDA leadership. He seemed preoccupied with my knowledge of current paramilitary affairs.

I began to feel uncomfortable about his questions and also because I was inside a drinking club for the first time that was the private domain of the UDA. I recalled there were two locked doors we went through to get inside the pub. I knew I couldn't get out without the permission of these two men seated at the table. My fate may well have in the hands of someone who was known as a violent man with a short temper. I remember thinking to myself that I didn't have anything to hide, but I wasn't really thinking about whether I would have to hide my own lack of religious identity. I started to feel a sense of fear building up. "Why, on earth," I began to wonder, "did I ever consent to come into this place?" I began to question my own judgment on this matter, but there was little I could do after I came inside the pub.

The three of us sat around a table. The two UDA men had several beers. I had only one, but after about an hour, I had to use the restroom. While I was away from the table, I could feel that they must be talking about me. Sure enough, when I came back to the table the first question was flat out: "Bill, are you a Catholic or a Protestant?" I should have anticipated this question, but I think I was overconfident about my status as a professor at Queen's

University, and that I was interested in the conflict only from an academic point of view. At any rate, I had to come up with an answer to the question.

My first reaction was a feeling of resentment. I didn't want to be sorted out as a member of either church. I could have lied and said I was a Protestant to remove the threat, but my answer almost surprised me because I didn't have time to think.

I said quickly, "My mother was a Catholic and my father was a Protestant and we never went to church." There was a long pause after my statement. But to my surprise, neither of them followed up with any more personal questions. If I would have told the truth, I would have said I was an "agnostic," but I doubted whether either one of them knew the word, and even after I had explained it, they wouldn't have accepted it as an answer to their question. I thought maybe they might have thought that "the agnostics" were a new singing group in town.

The fact that I had "shaved the truth" bothered me because it violated my own oath, "never tell a lie." But in retrospect it may have saved my life because if I would have hesitated, they would have suspected I was a Catholic, and who knows what may have happened then? Later I felt better about telling them something that wasn't the whole true, but it was the only time that I fudged on being honest in respect to my own religious background.

During most of my time in the North, people respected my privacy. But once in a while, their curiosity did show through. One sunny Sunday afternoon I was with a friendly group of middle-class Protestants up on the north Ulster coast about 40 miles from Belfast. There was an easy atmosphere in their back garden as the conversation turned to the question of my probable heritage. They knew I was a combination of Belgian, Swiss and German, but that didn't interest anyone. Without thinking too much, I volunteered the fact that my father-in-law was a Protestant minister, and that his surname was Banion. He had told me he thought he had Irish ancestors, but he wasn't certain about their history.

Immediately I noticed everyone in the group leaned forward with a new positive interest. They all seemed relieved as they assumed I must be the same religion as my father-in-law, but that would have been wrong. Yet with that small bit of misleading information, there were now smiles all around the table. They must have felt I was all right because I was "one of them."

One of the older men said he was pretty certain that "Banion" was an Irish Catholic name, but that maybe my father-in-law's ancestors were "soupers." Everyone smiled and nodded their heads. I was the only one who didn't know about "soupers." They explained that during the Famine of the 1840s, Catholics (who were starving) would come to home of Protestants and beg for food. The story was that Protestants (who were not starving) would offer them a bowl of soup if they promised to change their religion and become a Protestant. Everyone agreed that my father-in-law's ancestors must have "taken the soup."

Before the "souper" topic was discussed, the conversation had been very non-sectarian, but after they assumed I was a Protestant, the anti-Catholic stories and jokes began to flow. There was a new feeling that we were all of the same religious affiliation. Later in the afternoon, after several more glasses of wine, we all sang sectarian songs that highlighted how Catholics are brought up with the "impossible belief" that priests can forgive sins, and how all Catholics automatically followed the dictates of the Pope. I was rather impressed by my own ability to sing sectarian songs along with them. I had been in similar informal situations before where everyone was of the same faith. I had to be prepared to go "either way."

But there was another time when it was not a matter of just singing songs. It was a time when I was genuinely afraid. Political prison inmates in Northern Ireland were sometimes given home leave on certain holidays. The day before Easter Sunday one year, I got a phone call from a loyalist friend of mine named Bobby who I had met while visiting the main prison outside of Belfast. He asked if I would like to meet him for a drink. This was the first time I would meet him on the "outside." We did go for a drink, but there was an experience before we arrived at the pub that was very frightening for me.

Bobby and another prisoner (a huge guy I had never met) showed up at my apartment and asked if I wanted to go for a ride. I sat in the back seat of the rental car as Bobby drove at top speed out of Belfast to a remote area in County Down, about 25 miles southeast of Belfast.

We nearly had an accident because Bobby started driving the wrong way down a one-way street. He muttered, saying that they had changed the layout of the road while he was in prison. We soon entered a rural area that was far away from any farms or houses. I asked where we were going and Bobby said,

"Oh, you'll find out Bill." We left the paved road and traveled up a two-tire track trail to a deserted hilltop overlooking the Mourne Valley. It was beautiful, but I was completely lost. Bobby and his large friend in the front seat were quiet. I sensed they had agreed beforehand where the three of us were going.

We stopped at the end of the trail, got out of the car, and spread the wire on a fence so we get through and walk out into an open field. Bobby walked on one side of me while the big guy stayed close to me on the other side. It didn't feel like a good situation. I wanted to ask again where we were going, but I was pretty sure they wouldn't answer me. So, I just walked along with them.

There was some evidence that someone had been using this open area for a firing range, which made me wonder about a paramilitary connection. I got the feeling that people seldom came up to this remote area, at least people who were not connected to some unlawful group. But Bobby and the big guy seemed to know where they were going.

The other man with Bobby asked me if I knew a particular person by name that was probably a member of the IRA. I did not know the name. The big guy, who was standing very close to me, looked at me very carefully. I sort of looked away. I didn't know what to do.

Next Bobby said, "I bet you are wondering why we took you up here?" Trying not to show my fear, I said as nonchalantly as I could, "Yeah, I guess I was wondering." Without making eye contact with me, Bobby looked over the valley and said (with a sly laugh) "Some men in prison fantasize about beautiful women, but while I was in prison, I kept thinking about the spectacular view from up here looking down over the Mourne Valley. I decided I wanted to show you how beautiful it is."

After standing there for a few minutes looking over the valley, we crawled back through the fence again, got back into the car, and drove down off the mountain. A few miles outside of Belfast we stopped at a loyalist pub where Bobby told all his friends, "I just took Bill up to the top of the mountain so we could look over the Mourne Valley." They all laughed like they knew that it was an inside joke. I didn't ask them any questions. But I got the idea it must have been some sort of a test to see if I would trust them.

I think I passed, but I'm not sure.

Since then, Bobby has gotten out of prison and we have become good friends. We have never talked about that day up in that remote hilltop in rural County Down, but I think he knew I was really afraid after we crawled through that fence.

I had visions of me ending up in a short newspaper article with the lead: "Queen's University Professor Disappears."

I'm certain that if we ever did talk about it, Bobby would laugh because the joke was on me. He might have added with a twinkle in his eye, "Bill, you should really be more careful where you go, and who you go with."

4. Getting to Know Them

It's amazing how much one can learn just by listening to people's life stories. After spending a major portion of 14 years in Belfast, my personal contacts and circle of friends grew to the point that I knew more people there than I did back home in Oregon. Through my teaching responsibilities at The Queen's University of Belfast, I met and talked to countless number of young people. Some of them took me home to meet their parents. I went to several memorable birthday parties, an almost endless number of Sunday dinners, and many long evenings in the backrooms of towns and villages across the North.

My journeys around Belfast were usually by foot, despite the rainy weather. I wore out several pairs of shoes and an incredible number of umbrellas. Many a day I walked seven or eight miles in every area of Belfast, a city of nearly 350,000 people. I visited every neighborhood in the city several times, especially the small ones that were nearly surrounded by folks of an opposing religious tradition. By my count, there were 85 specific districts or small regions that were clearly either Catholic or Protestant. I made a map of the city with green and orange neighborhood markings. My friends from both sides loved to see my sectarian map of Belfast. Even the police were interested in how I had marked the neighborhoods.

I often took pictures of scenes that were typical of Belfast neighborhoods. There was also an attempt to capture in photos, the political leanings of folks that was very visible in their graffiti. In one particular area of East Belfast, where there was a very small Catholic area that was completely surrounded by Protestants. Because the houses were so close together, their points of view were side by side. I took a photo in which there were two, obviously opposing, pronouncements: "Fuck the Queen," and "Fuck the Pope." Only in Belfast could I photograph these two declarations a few feet apart. No one nearby seemed to think the contrasting statements were that unusual.

Many a time I could feel watchful eyes upon me as I ventured onto these narrow streets around the city. I made it a practice to stop people on the street and ask directions, even if I knew my way. My favorite question was to ask directions to the city hall. Asking that particular question was like announcing that I was a harmless tourist who was completely lost. Some folks would laugh at me and shake their heads as they pointed out how I could get to the city center.

My greatest assets were my American accent and my Belgian surname. I could never have gone in (or out) of these neighborhoods if I had an English accent, or if my name was obviously British or Irish. Generally, I could cut the tension by introducing myself and make reference to being a professor at Queen's University. One of the best moves I ever made was to print up 500 of those business cards (I mentioned earlier) that indicated I was a visiting professor of political science at The Queen's University of Belfast, complete with my street address and telephone number. I gave away three boxes of those cards during my years in Ireland. I was told repeatedly that no one ever gave out business cards in Belfast working-class neighborhoods, especially to shadowy figures who had paramilitary connections.

Some local people thought I was foolhardy telling everyone who I was, and where I lived, in a city where secrecy was so important. But my goal was to be well-known by as many people as possible. It would have been very easy to track me down. Some folks were utterly shocked that I would tell them where I lived. Those business cards gave me a lot of credibility with the locals, even with the police. Members of the Royal Ulster Constabulary (RUC) were especially interested in my business cards. I think they were amazed that I wanted them to know who I was. I noticed they always put my cards in their pockets.

But I did raise many eyebrows as I walked into working-class pubs where strangers were not welcome. I found out later that strangers just don't do that in Belfast. It was a good thing that I didn't know that at the time. Everyone stared at me as I took the long walk back to the men's room. Toilets in Belfast working-class pubs are not a showcase of cleanliness! Sometimes the "need" to use the restroom caused me to go into places no one would ever enter if they had a choice. After a few years in Belfast, I got to know which pubs had toilets that I wanted to avoid.

In these kinds of neighborhoods, I was always looking for ways to speak to local folks in a more informal fashion. So, it was really important to find out what name folks used to describe themselves, and the name they used for other people. Soon after I arrived in Belfast, I discovered there were basically four names used by nearly everyone to describe other folks around the province. Each name highlighted their home religious community, and the degree of intensity of their conviction: *nationalists, republicans, unionists* and *loyalists*. These words were used every day as a sort of religious/political/cultural shorthand to divide folks into two main bodies with sub-groups to indicate their probable degree of commitment. A few people I knew resisted using these words to describe themselves because they said they were "independents," but I noticed everyone kept calling them by those names, despite their reservations.

The following discussion of names may appear to be obvious to most people who live in the North, but it is important to clarify these words because they may be misunderstood by outsiders. To a great extent there was some general agreement on these terms as used by local folks. I had a fairly balanced description of each that I think would be widely accepted.

When Catholics spoke of being "Irish nationalists," they were usually seeing themselves as *moderates* who claimed all of Ireland as one country with a culture that included a multitude of religious beliefs, music, history, poetry, and language. "Nationalists" I knew, saw themselves as inclusive in that they wanted all the diverse groups to live together on the island. As a group they were dedicated to using only democratic means to achieve their goal. They looked forward to a peaceful future where Protestants, Catholics and dissenters would all have equal rights in a united 32-county Irish democracy that included the entire island.

Continuing on the Catholic side: "Irish republicans" shared the hopes of the nationalistic community with the added belief that a *force of arms* was necessary to "re-conquer" a non-sectarian, unified state. The major republican paramilitary group was the Irish Republican Army (IRA). It evolved throughout Irish history as a group that used military tactics to combat British imperialism and discrimination. These Irish rebels were also devoted to establishing an independent republican form of government, but they justified using an armed struggle as a necessary means in the process. There had been times when the IRA was of less importance, but since the late-1960s, it had become the most important military/political force in northern Irish politics. Sinn Fein, (pronounced shin fain) had recently become the largest republican political party in the North. Together, Sinn Fein and the IRA have advanced politically to become the main voice of the Irish Catholics in the six counties. The ranks of the IRA have always drawn heavily from the Catholic working-class, especially men and women who have experienced the discrimination during most of Irish history. In recent years, the IRA has been on a cease-fire order, but it is standing by in defense of democratic institutions in the North.

On the other side of the conflict, the most important unifying force for Ulster Protestants has been their fear that Catholics will take over Northern Ireland and merge the North and South into one unified Catholic Irish state, leaving Protestants as a small minority stranded in a situation that was unfriendly to their faith and nationality. Protestants see their membership in the United Kingdom today as the only way to avoid living in an Ireland dominated by the Catholic Church.

As a result of their fears, "unionism" is the most important political word for Ulster Protestants. Most political and cultural leaders see themselves as *moderate unionists* who are committed to employing democratic means in their electoral activities, but they have also engaged in wholesale tactics of discrimination against their Catholic opponents. Historically, unionists have been willing to use gerrymandered legislative districts and repressive economic power to build an authoritarian state with a partisan police force. In recent years, however, they have reformed their tactics. They now gloss over their past anti-democratic history as a necessary means in the past to keep the Catholics in a powerless position so they couldn't overthrow the state.

But maintaining the Union with Britain is still the single most important mission for Ulster unionists. Their largest unionist political party today is the Democratic Unionist Party (DUP). They constantly remind all Protestants that they should see themselves as loyal British citizens who enjoy all the privileges of living under the Crown. Fear of losing the Union is the main unifying factor among these unionists.

There is yet another band of Protestants who call themselves "loyalists." They subscribe to the basic principles of unionism with the added feature they are willing to use force to keep Catholics in check. Working-class members of a Protestant heritage constitute a large majority among loyalist groups. There are two major loyalist paramilitary groups: the Ulster Defense

Association (UDA) and the Ulster Volunteer Force (UVF). Together, these two paramilitary armies have been willing to use violence to maintain the British Union. Currently, Ulster loyalists are in a temporary peace mode, but ready to fight again if the Union is threatened.

When I was in Belfast, it was not uncommon for me to meet with loyalists and republicans in different places on the same day. As I went back and forth between the two communities, I was constantly aware of their contrasting temperaments. There was (and still is) a classic psychological difference between Protestants and Catholics. They each see themselves, and their futures in a very different light. I was always reminded of their separate and unique ways of seeing the world.

Irish nationalists and republicans have a unique kind of optimism. Even when they were beaten down in ghetto conditions, living in poverty with few resources, they had an expectation that conditions could be improved if they worked together. They had a sense of confidence that didn't seem justified. I had Catholic friends who had lived in squalor, but they told me they always had faith that things would get better.

But on the Protestant side, there was the opposite message: "Things are bad and they're getting worse." My Protestant friends were often in a defensive mode, worrying about the recent moves of Irish Catholics. Despite the fact that they had complete control over the security forces, there was detectable fear among most Protestants that they were slowly losing control over the province. Even middle-class Protestants seemed to worry a lot about their future.

Other than their personal views about what was to come, I found another (nearly sure way) of determining whether a person was a Protestant or Catholic. I could listen to the words they used to describe the place where they lived. My Catholic friends spoke of the "North of Ireland," "the North," "the six counties, or even "the occupied six counties of Ireland."

I met a Catholic man who always wrote out a long return address on envelopes that he mailed. He declared that he lived in the "six illegally occupied counties of Ireland." I asked him why he went to all that trouble on his return address. He said he just did it "to piss off" the Protestants at the Royal Mail office. I asked if that wasn't a bit dangerous to attract attention to himself, and he said he had already "been in prison twice and he didn't think they could do anything more to him."

Protestants are more conventional in naming their country. They speak of "Northern Ireland" with conviction or they use the ancient name of "Ulster," even though it includes only six of the original nine counties. Generally, words used by Protestants were more common among local people because their particular words were the ones that appeared on official maps, on radio, television, or in the major newspapers. Most people who wanted to avoid controversy would use the placenames of the Protestant community, in part because these official names were sanctioned by the government, and also because these names would pass in both communities without raising eyebrows. I used all the names, being careful to remember who I was with at the time. I often referred to the region as "the North" because it was the easiest term to use, and because most folks accepted it in a general conversation.

But perhaps the most noticeable verbal difference between the two communities, was how people pronounced the letter "H." Every Catholic I knew said it with a "haitch" sound. One British soldier told me the surest way to tell a person's religious background was to ask, "What comes after the letter 'G' in the alphabet?"

While all the natives of Northern Ireland pick up clues like these through casual conversations, Protestants were more likely to comment on specific language used, and they also seemed to react more cautiously to a new person with an unknown religious identity. I found that Protestants tended to be more concerned about Catholics being in their midst. Protestants were also quick to notice expressions such as the "North of Ireland," or the "Six Counties," because these words suggested that Ireland was not yet complete, and that someday all the parts will be unified into one country.

While all of these differences existed in a choice of words internally, I was interested to note how many other similarities there were to the United States. For example, the history of the Catholic Irish is very similar to Blacks in the United States. The civil rights movements in both countries sang the same songs and went out in the streets to demand equality. The position of Irish Catholics in the 1950s and 60s was not unlike that of American Black people in the segregated South. These people in both countries were beaten down, and had every reason to fear the repressive policies of the local police. There may have been little reason for either minority group to feel any optimism about their future, but unexpectedly, there was a sense of hopefulness that grew out of their struggles to gain some measure of equality and access to power. In both cases, there was a feeling that history was on their side – that their destiny was to gain power so they could overturn the authoritarian state that had held them down for so many years.

The situation for Ulster Protestants in that period also had a parallel in the southern United States. When civil rights protestors marched down the streets in both countries, the local authorities overreacted with gangs of police officers that unleashed brutal beatings. The police in the two countries made the same mistake of allowing television cameras to film the beatings. In each case, the TV images were flashed around the world. The legitimacy of harsh majority rule was put on trial as public opinion began to sympathize with the minority. In Ulster, as in the American South, there was a growing sign of pessimism among local law enforcement as the tables turned in favor of those who were seeking equality.

As the civil rights movements continued in both countries, those who held power at the beginning fell into a defensive position that continues today. They are both still trying to hang on to a past when they were in power. But down deep inside their movements, most observers can see that the old establishment has lost its momentum.

In addition to the shifting of power from one side to the other side in Ulster, I was also aware of differences between the "haves" and the "have-nots." I found that working-class people of both communities were the most honest political/cultural barometer in the six counties. They would usually tell me exactly how they felt and why. These were the folks who knew about the conflict through their own personal experiences. I noticed immediately that they were strikingly honest in their comments. Folks in working-class neighborhoods didn't mince words.

Middle-class people, on the other hand, were more careful to hide their hostile feelings behind proper grammar. Upper-income folks may have harbored equally one-sided sectarian attitudes, but they were rarely immersed in the conflict, so they didn't know it from personal experiences. I found that middle-class people whispered and down-played their hostile attitudes, while those in the working-class sectarian ghettoes spoke up loud and clear.

I also found there was a more cautious point of view among middle-class community leaders. I interviewed all the major political and religious leaders in the North, but I found their comments were also carefully stated so as to guard against anything that might come back to haunt them later if conditions changed. They didn't tell me anything they wouldn't tell a TV audience.

But rank-and-file loyalists, republicans, and police officers were less likely to self-censor their comments. They had lost comrades in the Troubles and they all had a personalized view of the struggle. The look in their eyes showed me how they felt. What they said may not have been "the truth," but it was the truth as they knew it, and it had shaped their views of the world around them.

After I had been in Belfast for a few years, I started to notice that these working-class people on both sides had more in common with each other than either of them had with their own respective middle-class. There was a "wall" between upper-income and lower-income folks in the city that is seldom discussed, but it is very important. In some respects, the *class division within each religious tradition almost equals the sectarian attitudes that divides the two communities.*

I knew multiple middle-class people on both sides who were very proud that they had no association with working-class folks on "their own side." It was also true that working-class people throughout the North boasted that they felt no connection to what they called the "fur coat brigade" of the upper echelons of their own community.

Whenever the issue of paramilitary activity came up, I noticed that middle-class and upper- class people on both sides wanted to change the subject. People in the leafy suburbs had a noticeable disdain for the folks of their same religious background who were doing the fighting and dying. They didn't want to know about paramilitary leaders on either side, and they certainly didn't want to claim them as part of their own community.

Early on, I found that working-class people from both sides had many things in common with each other. The personal stories of rival paramilitary members in both communities were remarkably similar. They grew up in poverty and knew what it was like to drop out of school because they had to get a job and help support the family. Contrary to public expectations, I found most paramilitary leaders had a real sensitivity for the people living in the red brick row-houses on their side of town. In many cases, paramilitary leaders represented working-class folks better than their elected representatives in the government.

Sinn Fein President Gerry Adams grew up in a besieged republican neighborhood of Ballymurphy in Catholic West Belfast. He joined the IRA at age 16 and soon after became a bartender in the Duke of York, a small downtown pub down a narrow city-center alley. Martin McGuinness, Chief of the IRA, left school at age 15 and worked as a butcher's helper in Derry.

David Ervine, head of the Ulster Volunteer Force (UVF) joined loyalists' groups at an early age. He grew up in the working-class section of East Belfast near the shipyards. I knew Ervine's brother and mother well. They were a close family that struggled to make ends meet. Despite David Ervine's lack of formal education, he was exceptionally bright, and had an extensive vocabulary. Some of his friends jokingly told me they thought "David had swallowed a dictionary." Raymond Smallwoods of the Ulster Defense Association (UDA) and I were quite close. Ray was a natural leader and had joined a loyalist organization as a teenager and rose up through the ranks to be the spokesperson for the largest Protestant paramilitary group in the North.

If it had not been for the sectarian division, these working-class leaders on both sides would have gotten along quite well. They had a lot in common. They knew what it was like to be near the bottom of society. All the ones I knew were very intelligent and had natural leadership abilities, but each of them had blue-collar worker roots that were much the same on both sides of town.

These class lines were similar to my working-class students at Queen's University. While they were scheduled to earn a university degree, they told me they still felt their working-class origins would hold them back. There was a class-consciousness among working-class folks from both communities that gave some of them a sense of inferiority. I spoke at length about this with my students and friends, saying that there was no limit to what they could achieve, but it remained as something that each of them had to overcome on a personal level.

As I moved around the many neighborhoods of Belfast, I was constantly aware of how much working-class people had in common, and I wondered repeatedly why they were thrust into an armed conflict against each other.

One of my earliest questions was why didn't working-class people on both sides see the value of banding together in a cross-community labor union? It just seemed natural that they would get together and organize for better wages, working conditions, and housing. Why did they not cross the sectarian divide and negotiate as a cross-community unit with management to gain a better life?

But I soon discovered a political/economic partnership that has haunted Belfast for many years. Upper income business leaders on both sides had something in common: they wanted to block labor unions that would include folks from both sides. Protestant business leaders warned their rank-and-file workers that "the Catholics will take your jobs if you let them." Economic leaders on the Catholic side warned their followers that you "can never trust the Protestants."

Surprisingly, most everyone I knew didn't think there was any hope for cross-community organizing. They kept saying, "maybe later when the guns are put away." But from my point of view, a union that included folks from both sides of town might serve as the best example of how to work toward peace. If Catholics and Protestants belonged to the same labor union, that in itself would be a reason to put the guns aside. I always thought that a secular labor union might be the single most important step in reducing hostile feelings in the North. Each side had a long labor union tradition, and both sides had many of the same economic problems.

I went to many labor union meetings on both sides and I kept bringing up the prospect of uniting working-class people. I kept hearing the same message. It had been tried before and it didn't work. After a while the men at the union meetings on both sides got to know me. They must have wondered why a professor from Queen's should be so interested in combining labor unions.

The inability to organize across the divide was true with a long list of workers and/or professions. Teachers did not have associations that combined both sides, nor did construction workers, journalists, mail carriers or city workers. Even garbage workers were divided into special crews for each religious community. Because of safety concerns, they generally refused to pick up garbage in opposing neighborhoods. The "green crew" went into Catholic neighborhoods and the "red crew" worked in the Protestant part of town.

One of my best friends was May Blood (1938-2022). She was the daughter of a Protestant labor leader in Belfast who tried to organize Catholic workers in a cross-community union. May's childhood home was burned down by fellow Protestants who wanted "no part" in a union that would include "Fenians." She told me they simply refused to sit down at the same table with union members from the other side.

May Blood worked on cross-community peace projects, women's issues, and union organizing all her life. She was rewarded by being appointed to the British House of Lords in London, but she never lost her common touch. She seemed uncomfortable when others noted her prestigious title. Her comment to me was, "just call me May." She always had time to talk about ideas that might bring people together. Her efforts were appreciated by folks who supported progressive causes throughout the North.

Everyone knew there were invisible barriers between the two communities that kept people apart. There was one group, however, that I thought could work together. But in the end, it turned out I was wrong.

One evening I attended a public meeting of Belfast Atheists. It was billed as a forum to discuss the topic of teaching religion in schools. Naturally, everyone there was opposed to religious education of any kind. After the formal meeting ended, I was invited to join about 10 of them to meet at a nearby pub. It was a jovial group. They began our conversation by personally introducing themselves around a large table. I took special note of their surnames and addresses; they all sounded like they had Protestant surnames and lived in Protestant neighborhoods. I asked the sensitive question: "Where you all born into Protestant families? It turned out that everyone at the table had been born a Protestant. I then asked if there were any former Catholics who were atheists. They said, "Oh yes, there are Catholic atheists, but we couldn't get along with them. They have their own separate organization."

Later in the conversation, I asked this group of atheists whether they still felt an association with other Protestants in the North, despite the fact they didn't believe in God. One guy with a resigned look on his face shrugged his shoulders and said, "Oh yea, in Northern Ireland we'll always feel we are Protestants, that won't change, no matter what we really believe.

5. Why They Fight?

My first plan when I arrived in Belfast was to talk to people that have been "involved" in the conflict and hear their individual reasons for opposing folks who lived on the other side of town. I guess I expected to get sets of personalized views that would make sense of why this sectarian war could not be resolved. Perhaps there would be a recurring theme that would provide me with a working-idea of why each side was fighting the other.

But before I had the opportunity to talk to any people in working-class neighborhoods, I started to notice all the colorful murals on their building walls. Could these painted symbols and slogans supply clues why the two sides have been locked in a struggle for so many years? It was impossible to overlook the opposing cultures in the paintings that proclaimed warlike doctrines about attacking and defending their neighborhoods. I had never been in any place that had so many visible images of a deep division that had existed for so many decades. I could feel pent up anger in many parts of the city, but there was a difference between the two communities that told me a lot about how each group saw itself, and why both had a bunker mentality about their futures.

On the Catholic side of Belfast, there were pictorial stories of famine, suffering, and a hunger strike where ten men died voluntarily in prison. There was a consistent theme in these republican murals of a people who had been in chains for generations, and their eternal struggle to be free. Some of the wall paintings were religious, others were cultural, but there was always an additional quality of historical sadness in each of the images. There was an added reminder of political affiliation: the curbstones in these neighborhoods were all painted green, white, and gold.

In Protestant loyalist neighborhoods the dominant symbols were more militaristic. There were soldiers in battle dress with guns, signs of victory in armed conflict, and the Union Jack was everywhere. It was clear that the Protestants were expending a lot of their energy in defending themselves. There were stories on their walls on how they had been tested in battle many times, but behind it all was an underlying lack of security – their backs were up against the wall – they were unsure of their future. All of this plus the curbstones were painted a bold patriotic red, white, and blue.

But the question was still in my mind, why were there paramilitary units from both sides on combat missions around the city? Was it basically a culture war that featured two stories of insecure people who felt eternally threatened by their neighbors? If so, what was the ultimate goal for each? What did the leaders have to say was the reason for conflict?

On the Catholic side, the reoccurring leader's proclamation was to unite Ireland (North and South) under one republican government. The overriding implication was that the island was obviously meant to be one nation and the British government had to be removed so the Irish state could be restored. The unofficial national anthem said it clearly:

> A Nation Once Again,
> A Nation Once Again,
> And Ireland, long a province be
> A Nation Once Again

In fact, I was to find out later, Ireland had never been unified under one government of any kind until the English imposed colonial rule on the island. It is one of those things not mentioned by the Catholic Irish who love to see their struggle as *restoring* an all-Irish government that never existed in an official form, but, according to the leaders, the *reunification* of North and South remained as their main goal.

From the Protestant political leaders, the focus was to recognize the international border between North and South, and maintain British rule in the North. The Union with the United Kingdom was an almost sacred feature in the Protestant psyche. Even though the ties with Britain seemed secure, Unionists in the North were obsessively reminding themselves of their political, cultural and religious ties with their mother country.

Again, it was through the music that one could understand why Protestants were willing to fight. The most widely-known Protestant loyalist song was, and still is, *The Sash My Father Wore*. The opening words of the song say it in a memorable way. Every Protestant in the North (young and old) is familiar with the tune. It has been the main marching song in Orange parades for countless generations. The melody is heard across the province during every summer:

> Sure, I'm an Ulster Orangeman, from Erin's Isle I came.
> To see my British Brethren all of honour and of fame.
> And to tell them of my forefathers who fought in days of yore.
> That I might have the right to wear the sash my father wore.

Imagine the Orange marches with hundreds of men in black suits, bowler hats, white gloves with orange sashes around their shoulders – carrying the Union Jack – all marching in step as they look straight ahead in a determined manner. In Protestant neighborhoods their parades were greeted by throngs of smiling people, clapping to the cadence of the music. But when Orange marches went through Catholic republican neighborhoods, the sounds from the onlookers were cursing, obscenities, and demands to "get those Orange bastards out of our neighborhood."

It took me awhile to grasp the importance of wearing the Orange Sash. Finally, I came around to the understanding that it was a symbol of British citizenship in Ireland – it was a proclamation that they were members of the British Empire – that their relationship with Britain was eternal.

I was impressed by the symbols, music, and marches by both sides all over the province, and the declarations made by political leaders, but there was still another level of analysis about *why the people fight*. There were amateur historians in every pub who could quote chapter and verse, "what they did to us," and why we must be vigilant because they will try to do it again.

Catholics I talked to in republican pubs brought up the fact that the British had been trying to colonize Ireland for hundreds of years. They talked of Oliver Cromwell, who invaded Ireland in 1649, and was responsible for unspeakably cruel acts against the Irish people. Also noted were the colonial policies to discriminate against Irish Catholics across the land. There were many details given that seemed to justify Irish anger and resentment. The bottom line to rectify this shameful history was to cast aside British rule and unite all of Ireland under one republican government. I was told this was why Irish republicans were willing to fight.

In Protestant pubs I heard a lot about the massacre of innocent Protestants in 1641, when hundreds of innocent Protestants were killed by

Catholics in the town of Portadown. One guy even sang a song about how scores of people were tied up and thrown off a bridge to drown in the River Bann. He also recalled how hundreds of Protestants starved during the 105-day-siege of Londonderry in 1689 when an army led by Catholics encircled helpless Protestants inside the city walls. For Protestant loyalists, their collective memories from the past gave them the reason to fight on and to secure their union with the British in the future.

These atrocities of the 17th century etched terrible memories that were more than 300 years old, but they didn't pass the test in my mind. I asked myself again, did those violent stories really sound like the reason why nearly four thousand people in the 20th century were killed in a war that lasted nearly 40 years? I was looking for a specific reason why someone would pull a trigger or set a bomb in place. I wondered what kinds of justifications would run through the mind of a person who was willing to kill folks that lived just down the street? It had to be something more compelling than the terrible historical events of the 17th century.

The question of "Why Do They Fight" was always on my mind. I spoke with scores of current and former members of paramilitary units. These were personal confidential conversations when we were facing each other, eye to eye. Without asking the question directly, I heard the answer again and again. Why we fight was a response to something that was more *recent and personal*. It was what "they did" to my father, uncle or my neighbor, or what "they did to me." The "reason" was drenched with personal anger and it motivated fighters with an eagerness to strike back.

It turned out that the *real* motives for military combat in Northern Ireland were basically the same as they are around the world. It all came down to what "they did" to someone that particular fighter knew. Terrible events of 300 years ago are brought up for public condemnation, but they don't motivate angry people like the events of the past week.

Perhaps the best example of this was a conversation I had with an old friend who had been involved in Irish republican affairs for years. We discussed why someone who faced arrest and long terms in prison would volunteer to fight and risk their life. My friend asked if I wanted to meet with some men who could answer my questions. We arranged that we would meet again at 8 pm four nights later at a taxi stand at the bottom of the Falls Road in West Belfast.

My friend and I took a taxi to a non-descript, very modest house off the Falls Road. We walked down an alley into a dark area that was some distance from the street. I was ushered into a dingy backroom of this small house where there were two young men I had never met before. They called me by my first name and seemed to know my background. I was a little put off because both of them wore scarfs around their faces. There were no "pleasantries" or greetings. My contact person left quickly after I sat down at a table. One of the two men said. "Bill, it's about time you get an education of what this war is all about."

The two men acted as though they had a connection to the IRA, although they never made that claim. They had several loose-leaf booklets packed with graphic accounts and pictures of people who had been tortured and, in some cases, killed by the security forces. There were pictures of people who had been shot and killed. Most of the material looked like it had been photographed from papers that had been folded many times. They said they were willing to meet me because, as they said, they wanted the world to know what "the Special Branch of the Royal Ulster Constabulary (RUC) had done in the Six Counties." There were several accounts of torture, of being locked up in a cage where they could not sit or stand-up, sleep denial, white noise that was piped into their prison cells day and night, and on top of this they were beaten on a regular basis. We spent nearly two hours going through all the material they showed me.

One of the men told me he had been blindfolded and taken up in a helicopter where they tried to push him out the door. He said he was terrified. Later that man found out the helicopter was only a few feet above the ground. There were cases of water-boarding, electric shock treatments, and torture. After hearing all the grizzly details for several hours, and seeing all the graphic pictures, I could feel the anger in the room. There was no question of what motivated them.

I never felt unsafe in the meeting because it was clear at the outset that the focus was on showing me the most dramatic evidence of how republican prisoners had been treated in the Special Branch integration rooms at the Strand Road RUC Station in Derry, and the Castlereagh Holding Center in

East Belfast. That meeting was all about why Irish republicans were fighting the war.

Later I had a similar meeting with several loyalists in a pub. They recounted a time when their best friend was killed while delivering free turkeys to folks in their community. There were accounts where the IRA had lined up Protestants along a rural road and shot them all in cold blood. In addition, they supplied the names of whole families who had been killed in a bomb that blew up a restaurant, and also police officers they knew on their street that had been shot by a sniper.

Neither side mentioned historical events. It was all recent – it was all personal.

6. Burdens They Carry

As I got to know more about the people in Ulster, I soon discovered that each side had a very complex set of issues that have weighted them down in the conflict. Both Catholics and Protestants had built-in handicaps and disadvantages that made it more difficult for them to achieve their goals.

First, I'll deal with the Protestants. I remember an older man from East Belfast telling me, "We love our mother, but she doesn't love us back." He was referring to how Ulster Protestants love being "British," but how there was little evidence that British society had much affection for them. The Union Jack flies all over Protestant neighborhoods in the North, but deep down these folks fear that they've become the stepchildren of the United Kingdom. Everyone knows that there's been a long series of British governments that have shown little support for the plight of Ulster Protestants who feel surrounded by Irish Catholics. But the Protestants of Northern Ireland continue to defend their place in the Union. "It's difficult to stay British when it's just a "one-way love affair," a woman told me. A lot of Protestants fear that London would be happy to cut their ties with Ulster and let the Irish people of the entire island fight it out among themselves.

One of my students at The Queen's University said he had read history extensively and concluded that Northern Ireland was just "a left-over" from British colonial history. He said it was "valuable at one time," but it was no longer as asset to the Empire. This young man said "The Brits will leave us behind some day just like they have with all the other colonies." As he was speaking, I noticed a certain coldness in his voice. He said he had been born a Protestant, but he had lost both his faith in his religion as well as in his country.

It is true, throughout history, Ulster Protestants have felt that British people "across the water" didn't really care if the Union Jack continued to fly over the province. Millions (perhaps billions) of British pounds have been spent defending the Protestant state from the Catholic Irish. But Northern Ireland has become something of a financial "black hole" for the Union as it sucks in millions of pounds each year. It costs the British taxpayers more of their hard-earned cash every year just to keep Ulster solvent. British citizens in Birmingham and Edinburgh are sick of hearing about the eternal problems in Ireland. Many of them just wish the conflict would go away.

On top of this, various British prime ministers and political leaders have launched a series of plans giving Irish Catholics more of a role in governing the North of Ireland. It was said that the British have spent decades pondering the "Irish Question," but then the Irish, secretly, would "change the question." So, the British never really understood the problem.

In recent years, London has even permitted the Irish government in Dublin to have direct involvement in northern Irish political affairs. This lack of resolve in London has made Ulster Protestants feel even more desperate in their fight to keep the Union Jack flying over Belfast City Hall.

I remember talking to the Reverend Ian Paisley, leader of the Democratic Unionist Party (DUP) about this subject. I questioned whether he could depend on the government in London. He shook his head seriously as he looked me in the eye and said, "They're a big part of the problem. I fear they will throw Ulster overboard into a sea of Catholics. We can never trust them."

I noticed a note of betrayal in Paisley's voice. Like a lot of other Protestants, he felt the loyalty had always gone just one-way. Ulster Protestants are proud to be British, but the folks across the water show no pride in their association with Northern Ireland. I've never seen demonstrations in London or Glasgow to show that the English or Scottish people loved their Ulster brethren.

It appears that folks in England, Scotland and Wales have a very disinterested view about Northern Ireland. I remember when a friend of mine was checking into a hotel in London. He wrote his address in Belfast as being in "Northern Ireland." The desk clerk commented on his address by saying, "Just put down Ireland, it doesn't matter what part, you're all the same to us."

Stories like this make northern unionists feel that they are the only ones who really care about defending the Union. They are quick to remind everyone that Ulster sent a crop of young men to fight in both World War I and II. The continuing theme among Ulster Protestants is that, "We have given so much, but we have received so little in return."

But in addition to the one-way loyalty problem, Ulster Protestants have a sense of self-destruction that also seems to be a part of their built-in burden they carry. Individually, they turn on each other at the drop of a hat. They're always splitting off into new subgroups. There's an old joke about these Protestants: "If you get two of them together, you'll hear three different political opinions."

But northern Protestants are actually proud that they disagree with each other on nearly every detail of life. They are eager to vote on every question and they debate many issues endlessly. One day I was walking in my neighborhood and came upon two Protestant people I knew well. They were involved in a long-drawn out disagreement on whether to use candles and organ music in their church. One man said it was forbidden in the Bible. The other person denied the biblical reference, but contended he opposed candles and organ music because it would make it appear that his church was too much like the Catholics. The first man countered saying he would no longer go to church if they had candles burning or if the singing was accompanied by the church organ.

The interesting point was they agreed with each other, but they ended their conversation in a very combative mood. I've never been around people who agree so clearly on the one big issue (keep Ulster British) but separate from each other so often on many other issues.

One of the mottos of northern Protestants is, "Not an inch." They are proud of standing their ground, it is part of their political identity. This sentiment surfaces again and again in public affairs when it's important to defend a position against overwhelming odds. Their tenacity is not only legendary in Northern Ireland, they have a reputation for courage in the United States as well.

Folks in the United States may not realize that Ulster has furnished America with many great folk-heroes. Frontier fighters like Davy Crocket, Sam Houston, Jim Bowie, and Daniel Boone have all come from Ulster stock. Twenty-three US presidents have claimed Irish heritage, twelve of that number came from what is now Northern Ireland. During the American Revolutionary War, General George Washington once proclaimed that if he had to make his "last stand," he wanted it to be with his Ulster-Scot soldiers. (These, of course, were people from Scotland who immigrated to Northern Ireland.)

When I mentioned this reference of the Ulster-Scots to a Protestant friend of mine he told me, "We don't hide or run away, we stand our ground and fight." That is a theme I heard again and again. The Ulster Scots are not afraid of a fight. This is evident in so many areas of life.

The celebrated Hatfield and McCoy dispute of the 1880s in the United States also has its roots dating back to this part of the world. The McCoys were Scots-Irish and the Hatfields were likely of Anglo-Saxon stock. It is a prime example of clan-type behavior that was transported into the Appalachian area of eastern United States. There is still today a lot of pride among Americans in being Scots-Irish. They are proud of their independent nature in religion and politics.

This heroic and uncompromising nature of Northern Protestants has been useful in clan disputes and warfare, but it is not an asset within their own community. Fighting among your own kin does not promote peace in the family. Many of the Protestants I knew in Belfast have stories about how quickly Ulster Protestants can turn against their own people. None of their leaders are safe from public ridicule. Even their clergy must be careful that their congregations do not rise up in opposition to them. Many ministers are "elected" to serve only for a one-year term. They can be discharged very easily by their own flock. One minister I knew said he felt like he was always "walking on eggshells."

The Right Reverend Samuel Poyntz, former Bishop in the Church of Ireland and I were good friends. We had many long sessions discussing the Protestant side of the conflict. Poyntz was visibly upset by what he termed as the "eternal squabbles of unionist politicians." From his point of view, this characteristic was a major hindrance to working for peace in the province.

Another Protestant clergy friend of mine was Reverend John Dunlop, former Moderator of the Irish Presbyterian Church. He stressed the fact that division and dissent had always been a feature of Irish Protestantism. He said that at one time in the 19th century there were five different branches of the Irish Presbyterian Church, all in competition with each other. He contended that Irish Protestants have never trusted their religious or political leaders completely – their cause has always been split into factions. A Protestant friend of mine jokingly told me that whenever Irish Protestants get together, the first item on the agenda is to split and form two independent groups.

Yet seriously, within their culture, there is the belief from the Reformation that it is "healthy" to break off from a church or political party and start a new one. Not surprisingly, there is a wide-spread pride in "protesting" against a larger body. This built-in distrust of working together has been responsible for many new religious groups being formed from a former church.

I checked the Northern Ireland telephone book not long ago and found that (by my count) there were 43 different churches in Belfast that had probably been born through some process of breaking away from a larger church. On the other side, of course, there is just one Catholic Church, which appears to be all-powerful. This situation has become more threatening for Protestants because Catholics, for the first time, now outnumber them in Northern Ireland.

These new population figures have caused some Protestants to become even more desperate. They've become even more critical of their own political leaders. Frequently there is a split off whenever there is even a minor disagreement. Catholics, on the other hand, are more inclined to avoid major breaks in their organizations. This point was made clear to me one day when I attended political meetings of each community on the same topic. What I noted that day illustrated that the two sides had a dramatically different relationship with their leaders.

During the early days of the peace process, there was a major question among Protestants on whether they should even talk to Irish nationalists before the IRA gave up all of their guns. David Trimble (1944-2022), leader of the Ulster Unionist Party (UUP), had increased his contacts with Catholics, but he carefully avoided giving in to any demands from the other side. I was standing close to Trimble when he finished his speech before a large group of his political party. I followed him out of the hall as members of his own party grouped behind him shouting "Trimble is a traitor – Trimble is a traitor." David Trimble faced harsh criticism no matter what he did. There was nothing he could do to please everyone within his own political party.

Later that same day, I attended a meeting of Sinn Fein members with two of their two major leaders, Gerry Adams and the late Martin McGuiness (1950-2017). The topic was whether to make contact with Ulster Protestants before Catholics would be permitted to enter into the proposed northern government. There were several Sinn Fein members who were critical of

Adams and McGuiness. But there were young men behind me that kept saying, "Give Adams and McGuiness some slack to negotiate with the Prods." After a short debate, there was a guarded agreement that Sinn Fein would open discussions with the unionists. Ultimately the group of Irish republicans stood with their leaders and took the risk to enter the talks. Closing ranks within their own organization has usually been a characteristic for Irish republicans. It seems likely that some of that centralization feature may have been inherited from the Catholic Church.

This practice of speaking with one voice is very prominent within the Catholic Church. In fact, the Church does not provide for *any* debate within its local ranks. It is basically a monolithic organization with a top-down structure. Decisions are made at the upper strata and passed down to those at the parish level. This concentration of power at the top has made it very possible for the Church to ignore the contending views of its local members. This has been a problem for Irish nationalists for many generations. There is no avenue for local people to challenge Church policies or doctrines. Some of the Catholics I know grumble about this constantly.

This insulation from rank-and-file members made it possible for the Catholic Church of Ireland to work closely with the British government, much to the displeasure of Irish republicans. The outside world is usually surprised to learn that Irish Catholic church leaders and the British government have had similar goals in Ireland for many years. They both wanted to maintain political and economic control over the Irish people. Neither of them wanted the Irish public to be influenced by progressive ideas or promoting more equality in community affairs.

Ironically, British leaders began to see the Catholic Church as a potential ally rather than as an eternal foe. Both of them opposed radical political movements that were spreading across Ireland. Neither of them wanted to deal with groups that advocated equality. The result was an unholy alliance than began many generations ago, and continues to this day.

To keep the education of Catholic clergy under isolated control, the English government agreed in 1774 to build and endow a seminary for Irish priests at a cost of "214,000 pounds sterling" each year.* The result was the development of the seminary at Maynooth, west of Dublin. It remains today as the major educational facility for Catholic priests in Ireland. It is still a bastion of religious and social conservatism. One priest I know called it a "conservative/theological boot camp" for the Catholic clergy. He added, "They don't turn out many progressive priests at Maynooth."

There was always a bone of contention between the IRA and the Church on the conduct of republican funerals. Usually, priests would not permit a uniformed IRA color guard to be present inside the church, nor did they allow the coffin to be draped by the Irish Tricolor flag because it was seen as a symbol of the republican movement. I have witnessed a bit of shoving and pushing between the republican honor guard and local parish priests. Usually, the local priest won out.

This is a sore point among many republicans who are still bitter about the "colonial ties" of the Catholic Church. I know many former IRA volunteers who are devout Catholics, but they strongly resent the political leanings of their own church. Some will only go to Mass if it is said by a priest who has the respect of the republican movement. In many localities there was a real division between the parish priest and local republicans.

Throughout Ireland, other Catholic priests were also expected to fall in line with Church leaders. An example of this came to my attention in a conversation I had with a young priest who said it was time to encourage rank-and-file Catholics to attend Protestant churches so they would get to know individuals from the opposing community in a friendly social setting. I will not name this priest for reasons that will be evident, but he told people in his parish to go to a Protestant church once a month instead of going to Mass. He said there was usually a short coffee/tea session after a Protestant service that was very relaxed. The priest said this was a great way for people on both sides get to know each other outside the confines of sectarian boundaries.

I thought this was a great idea and I mentioned it to Catholic cardinal Cahal Daly (1917-2009) during an interview. The cardinal leaned forward with an angry look on his face and asked me to give him the name of the priest. I said it was a "private conversation" and I didn't feel free giving his name. The cardinal was visibly upset as he persisted, "Is his parish in Belfast? Again, I declined as I got the feeling that the priest would have been in big trouble if the cardinal knew his name.

Cardinal Daly was known as being inflexible on most issues, he had a reputation for standing firm on all matters related to Church doctrine. I heard many stories to that effect from Dr. Eric Gallager (1913-1999), who had been the Moderator of the Irish Methodist Church, and who was also a strong advocate of integrating Ulster elementary and secondary schools. In recent times, approximately 90 percent of the children attended schools aligned with either the Catholic or Protestant communities. Dr. Gallager thought integration was a positive step toward peace and he brought up the subject several times with Cahal Daly, but the Cardinal would not even discuss the matter, nor would he explore the possibility of training Catholic and Protestant teachers in the same university. Gallager said Daly just turned his head away and would not even recognize integrated education as a legitimate issue.

Not surprisingly, Dr. Gallager said his most productive contact with the Catholic clergy had been with Father Des Wilson who had contacts with the IRA. At the time of our interview, Gallager said he was meeting with Father Wilson and agents of the British government concerning confidential negotiations in the peace process. Unlike Cardinal Daly, Dr. Gallager was willing to work with people from all sides. He truly wanted to cut through the rigid sectarianism that divided the two communities.

There had always been a gap between Irish nationalist leaders and the Catholic Church. There were several times when Church leaders publicly locked horns with the IRA. For example, Cardinal Daly and other Catholic priests questioned the moral stance of Irish republicanism during the Hunger Strike of 1981. Church leaders charged that members of the IRA on hunger strike were committing suicide which was a mortal sin. Republican leaders did not take on the Church on this point in public because they were afraid of losing support among Catholics in their ranks. But I knew former members of the IRA who voiced strong disagreements with individual priests.

In addition to the hunger strike, there were other issues that created a schism between rank-and-file Catholics and their Church. There was a public outrage against priests who sexually abused children. To make matters worse, there was proof that some bishops had moved the offending priests around to different parishes with no warning to keep them away from children.

Perhaps the most notorious priest in the North was Father Brendan Smyth (1927-1997) who was said to have abused nearly 150 children during a 40-year period. Smyth was tried and convicted and given a 12-year prison term. He showed no remorse for his actions.

When Smyth died in prison, *The Irish News*, the largest Catholic nationalist newspaper in the North, had a picture of Smyth on the front page with a headline above his picture, "Damn Him to Hell." None of the Catholics I knew in Belfast thought the headline was excessive in any way.

The child abuse issue has undermined the authority of the Catholic Church because there were several leaders in the Church (including the cardinal) who were responsible for permitting Smyth to continue his actions for 40 years. Even after Symth was charged, his religious order did not expel him from the priesthood. It was said by some Catholics, that Symth still had a car and that he drove around under cover as he continued his abusive actions.

There were other priests who were found guilty of similar offenses. I knew a young woman in Belfast who had a brother (who was a priest) who was also convicted of child abuse. He was placed in a cell that was totally isolated from other prisoners who threatened to kill him. I tried to interview him, but I was turned away by prison authorities.

In addition to the child abuse scandal, there has been a growing division between members of the Catholic Church on the issues of abortion, birth control, and divorce. The clergy in the South can no longer insist on church-related beliefs being enforced by the government in Dublin. There is an ever-widening gap between the people and their Church. In my own experience, I have witnessed a sharp decline among my friends who attend Mass, especially those who are under 30-years of age.

When I first came to Ireland, the attendance in Catholics churches was legendary. Some estimated that 85 percent of Irish Catholics went to Mass at least once a week. However, since the child abuse cases, a large number of Catholics no longer respect or trust the clergy. Now, much less than one-half of Irish Catholics attend Mass on a weekly basis. Catholic friends of mine still see themselves as members of the Church but they no longer attend Mass on a regular basis.

---

*Joseph McVeigh. *A Wounded Church: Religion, Politics and Justice in Ireland* (Cork: The Mercier Press, 1989). pp. 18-20.

7. Touts and Targets

One of my most important interviews in Belfast was with Gerry Adams, President of Sinn Fein (pronounced Shen Fain) which is the political arm of the IRA. He is the most respected person among Irish republicans today, and he is considered by many to be one of the main strategists of the Irish Republican Army (IRA). There were many Catholics in Belfast who viewed him as the man who united the republican community. I had been in Northern Ireland for several years before I got a chance to sit down with him and have a long talk.

It was common knowledge that Gerry Adams was a member of the IRA Army Council that made decisions on the conduct of the war. My only dependable knowledge of the Council was that it was made up of 6 to 8 members, that it was informal and made most decisions through consensus, rather than through a vote. I found out bits and pieces about the Council through a few people who had personal experience.

The British made every effort to break through the security of the Army Council so there was very little put in writing, and telephone conversations were held to a strict minimum. I heard one story about a time when members of the Special Branch broke into an Army Council meeting without warning. British agents stormed into the room and were grabbing everything is sight. The story goes that Adams had written down several points on a small piece of paper. Reportedly, Adams kept his cool and (in front of everyone) he lit fire to the piece of paper and used it to relight his pipe while he casually blew smoke rings. True or not, it's a great story.

When this tale was told in republican groups, there were laughs around the room. The implication was that Gerry Adams was their brilliant Irish leader, and the Brits (who thought they were so clever) never caught on that a small piece of paper might have had all sorts of critical information that would have aided British security forces against the IRA.

But the British did manage to recruit several individual IRA volunteers to become informers, or "touts" as they were called by Irish republicans. There were always rumors that the Brits had compromised some men at the upper echelons of the entire movement. There was so much speculation. The same names came up again and again.

For example, everyone knew that Martin McGinness, Gerry Adams and other republicans had meetings with the Brits that were not known by fellow republicans. It was during these years that IRA gunmen and bomb throwers were evolving into becoming Irish politicians and peace makers. Secret information and proposed plans must have been passed back and forth many times. At some point in the process, old enemies from Belfast and London began to work together toward the common goal of a ceasefire and finally a power-sharing agreement. I doubt if we will ever know for certain the role played by specific republicans or British government agents in the process.

But there were some principal players on the inside of the republican movement who surfaced as touts. In a strange twist of events in 2002, British intelligence revealed that a hard-core IRA man, Denis Donaldson had been working with their organization for 20 years. The alleged mole had been a close friend of both Gerry Adams and Bobby Sands. A republican I knew said Donaldson had recruited him into the movement. Several people said he was the most committed volunteer they had ever known. It later surfaced that Donaldson had become a paid agent during an especially "vulnerable" time of his life. Some speculated that he was protecting a family member, but no one I knew was certain why Donaldson had "turned." But after his public confession, Donaldson fled Belfast to live in a remote cabin in Donegal where he was tracked down and killed by Irish rebels who may (or may not) have been associated with the IRA.

Another equally important IRA man that became a tout was Freddie Scappaticci, also an early leader within the IRA. Scappaticci was a paid informant to a British intelligence unit for 25 years. His position within the republican movement was to track down informers and execute them. Reportedly, Scappaticci had a short temper; he acted with a vengeance as he killed scores of probable British spies within the IRA. There was speculation also that he killed some loyal IRA volunteers on orders from his British handlers. Scappaticci's British codename was "steak knife." Folks I knew speculated for years and wondered who was the disloyal figure behind the steak knife codename. The British credited him with giving some of the most important information during the Troubles.

I did not know either man, but I knew several people who knew both of them. The two men had very different reputations within the IRA. Donaldson was viewed as an inspirational figure by many. One person I knew said he "patterned his life" after Denis Donaldson, and that he was utterly shocked when his "mentor" confessed to working with the British. This person said the execution of Denis was justified, but he felt that Donaldson was protecting someone else through his actions. Some believed that Donaldson was still an "honorable man" despite his 20-year record as a British tout.

The other man, Freddie Scappaticci, was feared by a lot of IRA members I knew because he was in charge of the "nutting squad" that investigated everyone else. The name came about when it was revealed that suspected informers were tortured, then first shot in the head, and finally in the "nuts." Freddie, reportedly, was looking over everyone's shoulder. His job was to find disloyal members, force them to confess on tape, and then execute them. I never heard that he and the "nutting squad" were an inspiration to others.

In fact, one of my best republican friends was convinced that Scappaticci supplied the British with information that was responsible for providing evidence that sent my friend to prison. My former IRA friend spent many years wondering who knew the specific things that the British used as evidence in my friend's conviction. Needless to say, many mysteries were solved when Freddie surfaced as a long-standing British tout.

One of the things I learned about the republican movement in Belfast was that they watched a lot of people who didn't know they were being watched, including me. I was told that I was "never under any direct suspicion," but that I had attracted "a lot of attention" because I had so many contacts around the city with loyalists and the police. This old friend of mine said, "my behavior caused some people to wonder?" He didn't give me any details, but he said some people "kept their eye on me."

One of my former students at Queen's University once remarked to me "that I had to be one of the luckiest people who ever walked the streets of Belfast." He said that I was involved in "many close-calls" without knowing the circumstances. This person made that statement one Saturday afternoon in a neutral Belfast pub, and then refused to give me any details. To this day, I don't know what to think of his off-handed remark. It may have been the "drink talking" as they say in Belfast, or he may have known something that was unknown to me. At times, everyone in the province seemed to be watching and listening to everyone else. There were many secrets.

But the British did have an extensive state-of-the-art intelligence capability in the North that were designed to cut through the "secrets." Everyone I knew in Belfast who was "involved" assumed their telephones were bugged. We never referred in anyone by their proper name while on the phone – conversations were always devoid of detail. Individual users of telephones were constantly referring to the "other guy" without ever using real names. There were countless stories of microphones that could pick up conversations inside an automobile, and many devices were found in people's homes rigged inside electrical fixtures. In addition, there were closed-circuit surveillance cameras all over town. I went into nearly every police station in Belfast. They all had a cluster of monitors on the wall. The Brits never quit prying into everyone's life.

Helicopters hovered over some parts of town day and night. Low level criminals were given amnesty by the police if they reported on individuals on their street. Well-known republicans and loyalists were harassed and questioned at length. Some were arrested on trumped-up charges. A friend of mine was followed every time he drove his car to the grocery store. There were also late-night attacks on his home when the police would bang on the doors and shine bright lights into his bedroom windows. Some people I knew seldom slept in the same bed two nights in a row.

I asked Gerry Adams about the role of anger against the police tactics and the revenge motive within the IRA. He first of all denied that he was a member of the IRA, because the British had declared that all members could be arrested. He disagreed that anger played a role in republican operations. "Folks are not recruited into the IRA just because they are angry," he said. But he added with a crafty smile, "But the Brits do manage to stir up the pot pretty often, don't they?"

Gerry Adams and other senior republicans I have known often used the term "legitimate targets," suggesting that there were people that were targeted only because they were involved in the war." But in fact, that designation also included off-duty soldiers, police officers, government security workers, prison warders, food service people at police stations, and a whole host of people who had only a minimal part in the security operations. But the press reports from the IRA were usually careful to indicate that their targets were "legitimate."

But on the Protestant side there was little or no effort to be careful in target selection. I had a much greater insight into paramilitaries on that side and how they conducted their operations. I knew several leaders well and spent a lot of time with them in informal conversations. There was no equivalent of the Army Council on the Protestant side. There were two major loyalist paramilitary units that were in competition with each other: the Ulster Defense Association (UDA) and the Ulster Volunteer Force (UVF). Then there were offshoots like the Ulster Freedom Fighters (UFF), the Red Hand Commandos and several groups that floated around without a real name. Not only was there no unified command, in many cases there was intense competition between various factions. There were many intra-party disputes involving which unit was in charge in what part of the city. At one time, the UDA had eight separate commanders in Belfast alone. The cooperation between them was not uniform. In addition, many towns had their own separate paramilitary organization, and they jealously guarded their own local independence.

Also on the Protestant side, the Royal Ulster Constabulary (RUC) was basically a Protestant police force and many of its members were drawn from the same neighborhoods as the loyalist paramilitary members. Many of the police and the paramilitary members knew each other by their first names. Some UDA members I knew had tried to join the RUC, but they couldn't pass the entrance examination so they joined a local loyalist paramilitary unit instead. The RUC knew these men as neighbors and the police knew what was going on inside many of the paramilitary units.

A loyalist man I knew had been recruited by the RUC to kill three republicans in a town north of Belfast. The police furnished him with pictures of the three men to be killed, plus helpful hints as to where they worked, which pubs they went to, and the license numbers of their cars. This loyalist and his brother killed the three Catholics and they were arrested within hours by the same police officers that had given them the information. This person I knew was tried and found guilty and served 14 years in prison for first degree murder.

I told him later that he had been "set-up," but he denied it. I don't think he could accept the idea that he had been *used by the RUC* to murder three people he didn't even know. He told me he "knew what he had done and accepted the punishment." I told him that if I had been set-up, I would have been angry at the police. Later, we stopped talking the situation and he served his time.

Some Protestant political leaders had a personal relationship with loyalist gunmen. For example, one of the leaders of the UVF, David Ervine (1953-2007), told me that his group regularly coordinated their actions with the Reverend Ian Paisley, who was the founder of the Free Presbyterian Church, Head of the Democratic Unionist Party (DUP), and finally the First Minister of the Northern Ireland Assembly. There was a constant blurring between the legal and the illegal in Belfast. In many cases it was not clear who was ordering the gunmen.

Various illegal loyalist leaders I knew and legal political leaders were on a first name basis. It was an *open secret* that the police, the unionist political parties, and the loyalist paramilitary units often cooperated behind the scene. Their relationship was often disjointed, but it was there. I never heard anyone admit it in public, but I knew it was true.

In reality, a fair amount of the loyalist activities was spontaneous. Some guys just decided to go out and get a couple of Catholics. One afternoon I was meeting with a loyalist leader in a Shankill Road pub. The television set was on a news station and it showed a parade that was in progress on the Falls Road (a Catholic stronghold). Guys in the bar were watching the TV.

It wasn't long before the loyalists seated at the bar started shouting abuse and yelling about how great it would be to "stiff a Taig" (a derogatory name for killing a Catholic). Soon a couple of guys in the pub declared they were going over to the Falls Road. They took their beer with them as they stumbled out on the street. I'm not sure what happened to them, but there was a lot of cheering for them as they left the pub.

I've never seen anything even close to this on the republican side. The IRA was a very centralized organization. There were a few other competing republican paramilitary groups, but the IRA kept everyone in line. Their strength was based in part on their strategy of picking targets they thought would change the conduct of the war. Their plans were made behind closed doors by a few leaders who had "intelligence" on the opposition.

An example of this action was a calculated plan by the IRA, in the autumn of 1993, to wipe out the entire leadership of the UDA. The plan was to place one bomb below an upstairs meeting room where the UDA leaders were expected to meet at noon on a sunny Saturday in October. The operation was organized with two IRA volunteers, dressed as delivery men, who would bring in a box to the fish shop (under the meeting room) on the Shankill Road. The bomb inside the box was designed to blow upwards and kill everyone in the room above the fish shop. But several employees inside the fish shop caught on to the plan – they tackled the IRA members and the bomb tipped sideways and blew the front of the shop out into the street. Nine innocent people were killed who were walking or driving down the road plus the two IRA men who brought in the bomb. The IRA operation was a complete failure because the UDA leaders had left their meeting room early, so only non-combatants were killed. It was a terrible day in Belfast.

I happened to be in the Protestant neighborhood when the bomb was detonated and I was in front of the smoking remains of the fish shop within minutes after the explosion. It was a tragic scene. There were bodies and wounded people everywhere, and there was immediate anger and a cry for revenge. People I didn't know made eye contact with me and yelled obscenities in my face. I was careful not to say anything because I wasn't sure what they would think about my American accent. Without being told, everyone knew the republicans were responsible. I stood in the middle of a throng of people shouted their unprintable oaths to get even. Within hours everyone in Northern Ireland knew about the "Shankill Road Fish Shop Massacre."

For an entire week, republicans in the six counties waited for the response that everyone knew was coming. People in the Catholic working-class neighborhoods were especially worried. Everyone was nervous. The streets were empty at five o'clock each afternoon. When a stranger walked in off the street into a business or pub, most everyone present turned around in fear.

At the time, I was living in a community of 12 people in North Belfast, made up of Catholic and Protestant clergy. I was the only lay person in the two-house compound. I was not affiliated with folks of either religion. But because this small community had a reputation for welcoming people of both faiths, we were worried that we might become a target for loyalists who disapproved of our ecumenical practices.

Sure enough, a man called within hours of the Shankill Road bombing and said, "I'm going to come and kill all of you." We had to take the threat seriously. It was the one time I had to plan what I would do if I heard gunfire downstairs. There was a small closet behind the upstairs bathroom that I thought might be overlooked by a gunman who wanted to get all of us. But the threat never materialized. Yet we had to prepare a plan of what we would do if we became a target. From that day on, we knew that we were considered to be a "target" in some people's mind.

The real act of revenge came on October 31st when a small group of masked loyalists walked into a Halloween party in a nationalist pub in the small village of Greysteel (north of Belfast). The intruders with guns yelled "trick or treat." A woman at the bar said, "That's not funny." She was the first to die as the loyalists shot and killed seven people, six Catholics and one Protestant. It was a tit-for-tat killing to even up the score after the Shankill Road bombing. Everyone knew it was coming, it was just a matter of where and when.

As stated earlier, the IRA declared that their killings were all "legitimate targets" such as police officers or known paramilitary members. Loyalists, however, often engaged in what they called "representative killings" whereby they chose their targets at random with no thought of who these people were. They often boasted that "any Catholic would do." One particular loyalist said in an interview that he would drive through a Catholic neighborhood looking for a target, and would aim at one person, and then change his mind, at the last minute, and kill someone across the street.

The result was that *no one felt safe.* Young and old were afraid to leave their homes. During these times, the war had degenerated into a "blood feud" of rival gangs who seemed to enjoy the killing. There was one gang called the "Shankill Road Butchers" that picked up victims off the street, tortured them, and then cut them up into pieces. It was a time of real terror in Belfast. People with no political involvement became targets because they were walking down the wrong street at the wrong time. The leader of the Shankill Road Butchers gang was Lenny Murphy (1952-1982) who was a loyalist who wanted to prove that his Catholic nationalist surname did not determine his political views. Lenny Murphy was later killed by the IRA.

It was at times like this that the conflict was totally out of control. Everyone felt that they could be a target. People were even being killed in the leafy suburbs that were usually outside the conflict zones. During this time there were people killed watching football games in pubs, and farmers who were killed driving their tractors out in the field.

I remember watching a local television program during these times. Folks were interviewed from both religious communities as they discussed the daily fear of sectarian violence. One woman, who was interviewed, said she had a little bottle of pills up on the shelf, and whenever things got really bad, she would take a "wee Valium" to help her get through the day.

The surprising things about mental health at this time was that suicide rates declined during the worst days of the conflict. Sociologists noted that individuals had a greater sense of group identity when their community was under threat. The speculation was that the continuing conflict caused them to shift their attention away from their own mental health problems. Sadly, the reverse of this situation occurred when suicide rates nearly doubled after the ceasefires in 1998. Since then, young Ulster people especially, have had the highest suicide rates in the United Kingdom. Portions of Northern Ireland have become very depressing for folks who feel they have no future.

So, the human cost of the Troubles continues to take its toll among folks on both sides of town even after the guns have been put away. Lives were lost for no reason except that some people happened to be in the wrong place when orders were given to "even up the score."

So often in Ireland, it was the song writers and pub musicians who seemed to understand the true nature of the conflict, *There Were Roses* was a song with lyrics written by Tommy Sands in South Armagh about two friends who were killed at random. (Allan Bell was a Protestant and Sean O'Malley was a Catholic.) There was a phrase in the lyrics about those who ordered the killings:

An eye for an eye was all that filled their minds.
And another eye for another eye till everyone was blind.

The song, *There Were Roses*, can be heard today in a video on *Google*. In a few minutes, one can see and hear the reason why some of the northern Irish were caught up in the conflict. First read the lyrics and then listen to the music. What else is there to say about the inhumanity of targeting innocent people and seeking revenge.

8. Other Sides of Ireland

When I first arrived in Ulster, I did not know a single soul, but I did have the name and telephone number of Alf McCreary in Belfast, who had been the Northern Ireland reporter for the *Christian Science Monitor*. I called him late in the afternoon on my first day in town and told him I had been given his name by a fellow-journalist in Oregon. Alf McCreary's response was an offer from him and his wife to take me to a stage play that evening in Belfast. Their hospitality on that first day has continued for more than 30 years.

Throughout that time, Alf McCreary had been a working journalist for the *Belfast Telegraph,* and an advisor to the Vice Chancellor of The Queen's University of Belfast. In that capacity, he was a major leader in the Ulster educational and intellectual establishment. Throughout Northern Ireland, he had a reputation of being a moderate Christian conservative with a kind heart. Alf has written more than 25 books on Northern Ireland and is respected today as a person who understands Protestant middle-class culture in the North.

Over a 14-year-period, I had a standing invitation from Alf McCreary and his wife Hilary to dine at their home every Saturday evening. They became my family away from home. I got to know their three children, and I was included in various family and neighborhood celebrations. On our regular Saturday evening meetings, we always sat in the same chairs in the livingroom. Right beside Alf's chair was a framed display of his father's military decorations from World War I. It was clear that Alf was proud to be British.

Alf and Hilary were pillars of Belfast society. In addition to his university and newspaper work, Alf had a Sunday morning radio program on the local BBC station that explored religious topics. Nearly everyone in Belfast knew his name. In his capacity as a media person, he was on a first-name basis with mainstream Protestant religious and political leaders throughout the North. He and his church leader friends focused on a "gentler side" of Protestant religion and culture. I interviewed many of them and benefited greatly from their insights and friendships. They were a well-educated, friendly group of men and women who didn't talk of the conflict unless someone else brought up the subject, and then they focused on how unfortunate it was that the people of Northern Ireland were locked into what appeared to be an endless conflict.

Through the McCreary family and their friends, I gained a tremendous amount of respect for the moderate Protestant community that had been in Ireland for several centuries. Their ancestors came over from Scotland and England generations ago, and most of them had to struggle to make a living. Northern Ireland is dotted today with old churches and grave yards that are a testament to the tenure of these Irish Protestants. This particular group of British people see Ulster as their homeland. They feel they belong here.

Alf and Hilary McCreary and their friends had an appreciation of Ireland (North and South) that was outside the sectarian conflict. They knew what was going on in the blighted parts of working-class neighborhoods, but they chose to focus on other things that were special to them. It was through this kind of thinking that I learned of another side of Irish life that was more common to the middle-class Irish of both religious communities. They developed a rich heritage of their own that was colorful and unique.

An example of this was when several of us attended a meeting of local Protestants who honored the music of Percy French (1854-1920). This beloved character was an Anglo-Irish composer who was born in County Roscommon, the privileged son of a Protestant landlord. His music focused on the whimsical side of Irish culture where there was a wonderful make-believe part of Irish life. He clearly had a warm affection for the Irish people and how they lived. His tunes from the early 20th century would put a smile on the face of rich and poor alike. When folks listened to and sung his music there was always a twinkle in their eyes. I recall the humor and the laughter that was present whenever his name came up. There was something enchanting about sitting in a circle and singing the Percy French traditional ballad, *The Mountains of Mourne*.

The song tells the story of an Irish man who went to England, but who missed the mystical charms of rural life in County Down where the Mountains of Mourne "sweep down to the sea." In this song, French took delight in poking fun at the industrious people of London who were "diggin for gold in the street," while he idealized the unspoiled rural life in Ireland. Percy French was popular with folks who saw themselves as being Anglo-Irish, and who had a special place in their hearts for the native Irish. There was a poignant quality in his music that made people all over the world wish they were Irish. (Google the *Mountains of Mourne, read the lyrics* and listen to the enchanting music)

I saw no hint of division in the Percy French music, just a vision of a beautiful green place that transcended sectarianism. Certainly, he knew of the plight of the Catholic Irish, but he chose to focus on other things. I could see that it would have been easy for Ulster middle-class Protestants to become Percy French fans, and gain some relief from the dreary realities of the Troubles.

Much of the affection for Percy French is centered around the town of Newcastle, nestled in County Down at the foot of the "Mountains of Mourne." The Percy French Inn is on the grounds of the Slieve Donard Hotel, an up-scale hotel in the heart of Newcastle. The whole complex is the pride of Irish Protestants who gathered in this part of Northern Ireland for years to escape the dangers inside the working-class districts of the North. (The folks at the Slieve Donard Hotel even use the word "escape" in their advertising appeal for people to come to their hotel.)

Knowing this, the Irish Republican Army (IRA) bombed the Slieve Donard Hotel in what they called a "prestige-target bombing." It was designed to hit a symbol of middle-class Irish Protestant culture. According to one of my sources, one bomb was set to completely destroy the main dining room and grand staircase in the hotel reception area. This grand staircase had been the photo backdrop for countless middle-class family pictures during many years. My source said it was the same rationale that was employed in bombing the Grand Opera House and the Europa Hotel in downtown Belfast. There was one particular bombing in early December which made it necessary to cancel the Christmas program for that year. The *Belfast Telegraph* newspaper could not understand why the IRA had chosen those two targets. Why, "just before Christmas?"

Everyone knew that the bombings in Belfast were aimed at the Protestant middle-class and the upper echelons of the British establishment. Both targets were primarily "British Protestant" in nature in that they represented the British ruling class. It was a way of disrupting the lives of folks that did not live in the working-class neighborhoods. Spokespersons on local television and radio commented that the IRA had "no soul" or appreciation for the "finer things in life," that they were "brutes" who were destroying the Christmas season for their own "selfish goals." In return, the IRA announced that they were responsible for both bombs with the knowledge that they were striking at a part of life that many thought should be off limits during the war.

Most everyone who lived in Belfast knew that there were certain facilities, buildings, and events that generally "belonged" to the people of one cultural community. Paramilitaries tried to hit targets that were in the domain of the opposing community. But, at a lesser level, there were some places that attracted people from both sides. One of these were movie theaters in the city center that showed popular general-interest films that drew in young people from all over the city.

At the beginning of the conflict, owners of many theaters were loyal to the British monarchy and they instituted a practice they must have thought was patriotic. At the end of every movie, it was the custom in these theaters to play the British National Anthem. All theater-goers were then expected to stand in respect. This, of course, was unacceptable to Catholic patrons.

To avoid the practice of standing at the end of a movie, Catholics I knew would occupy the aisle seats so they could get up near the end of the movie and run up the isle and out the door before the Anthem was played. Knowing this, Protestants would come to the movie early and occupy the aisle seats to block any Catholic who tried to escape before the Anthem was played. This was a sort of game that was played mostly by young men and boys who pushed each other around for the sake of their community. As far as I know, no one was injured, but it did demonstrate the conflict was never out of mind. It was a "semi-serious" practice that was played out most Saturday afternoons in a few theaters that were located in the neutral area of the city center.

The city center was also the place where there was another so-called "rule." There was an unwritten understanding in downtown Belfast pubs that no one could talk about religion or politics. One of my favorite pubs in Belfast's city center actually drew in both Protestants and Catholics – a rare thing in a society where 25-foot walls separate neighborhoods by religious tradition. But in this particular establishment, men and woman from the

Protestant Shankill Road could sit down and share a peaceful pint with a Catholic who was born and raised on the Falls Road. These two roads in West Belfast are the main strongholds of opposing sectarian tribes.

Those particular conversations in neutral pubs reminded me of how civil the northern Irish can be in delicate situations. There was an expected unique behavior pattern in pubic when strangers interacted with each other. It was a matter of civil manners that folks avoided talking about religion or politics until they were certain they are among their own kind.

Early in a conversation many people would "tip their hands" by letting others know by subtle means whether they were Catholic or Protestant. One of the easiest ways was to mention the neighborhood they lived in or the school they attended. Many neighborhoods and schools were voluntarily segregated according to religious traditions, so finding out where a person lived or went to school was a nearly certain indicator of whether they are a Catholic or a Protestant.

But there is one pub in Belfast, however, where nearly everyone feels comfortable regardless of their religious membership or national identity. Perhaps the Crown Bar is the best-known pub in Belfast for tourists and local folks. It stands out in the city center on Great Victoria Street because it is a very ornate building with stained-glass windows. But the location of the Crown Bar has always been a problem. It is right across the street from the Europa Hotel that was bombed repeatedly by the IRA. The windows at the Crown were sensitive to nearby bomb blasts and they needed repair many times during the Troubles.

Yet despite the bomb blasts, the sophistication of the Crown continues when one steps inside. One whole side is devoted to a series of ten "snugs" that are booths with doors that permit small groups of patrons to have some privacy while they dine and drink. The whole interior is carved mahogany with gas lamps hanging from the ceilings. *Google* the "Crown Bar in Belfast interior photos" and "Crown Bar wooden snugs" to enjoy one of the classiest pubs in Belfast.

But the real claim to fame for the Crown Bar (from my point of view) was a young man who I call a "sectarian entrepreneur" who moves around the patrons in the Bar offering to tell five Catholic or five Protestant jokes for a fee of five pounds. Each joke is tastefully told and should offend no one. He is a modern example of how a person with business sense can capitalize on a sectarian conflict that has gone on for hundreds of years.

The longer I was in Belfast, the more I discovered how many sides there were to this conflict.

9. Covering the War

I developed a life-long friendship purely by accident with an Irish journalist in Belfast who worked every day in the middle of the conflict. Johnny Coughlin was a camera man for *Raidio Teilifís Eireann* (RTE) the largest radio and television company in Ireland. The main broadcast studios were in Dublin, but RTE covered Northern Ireland news on a daily basis. Johnny moved to Belfast at the beginning of the Troubles in 1968, and covered every political event up through the launching of the power-sharing agreement of 1998. He had more personal contact hours with the Troubles than any person I knew in the North.

I got to know Johnny through his daughter, one of my students at Queen's University who volunteered to come to Oregon to work on a political campaign. This came about when I announced at the end of my lecture one day, that my wife and I would help any students who wanted to come to the United States to work on a political campaign. I assured my students that they would be welcomed to work on Nancy Peterson's re-election campaign for the Oregon House of Representatives. Nancy was a friend of mine and I knew my students would learn a lot about Oregon politics from her. Two young women came up and expressed an interest, and it wasn't long before they arrived in Oregon.

One of the young women introduced me to her parents, Johnny and Geraldine Coughlin. We became friends immediately. When I was in Ireland, I spent a lot of time with Johnny in his RTE television office in Belfast. I frequently went out with the TV crew to cover the events in both loyalist and republican neighborhoods. We covered riots and funerals, and most everything in between.

I soon discovered that every day for television journalists was unpredictable. Often when there had been a bombing, a shooting, or a funeral, local people were emotionally upset. If neighborhood folks were looking for a way to express their anger, Johnny and the television crew were a ready target. In that capacity, it was a dangerous job. Johnny and the TV camera on his shoulder made him a marked man.

There was no affiliation name on Johnny's camera or clothing so local people could not tell if he worked for a TV station they disliked. People would often ask him which TV channel he worked for. His usual response was a vague statement "Oh, I work for the other station." Surprisingly, that usually satisfied inquisitive local persons until he could escape.

Our TV crew tried to maintain a low profile, as we watched the events unfold all around us. I seldom spoke, but when I did, my American accent sometimes drew unwelcome attention. In one particular case, my accent nearly got me in serious trouble. It was at an IRA funeral of a young man, Pearse Jordan, who had been killed by the police. His car had been stopped, and he was shot in the back by police officers as he was running away. Pearse Jordan was not armed, but the police contended he was a member of the IRA, and therefore he was a legitimate target.

The circumstances of the shooting were still being discussed on the day of the funeral. As was the custom in Ireland, the dead body was inside the Jordan home. The police surrounded the Jordan house to block any show of IRA support or solidarity. The father of the deceased young man was angry, and he refused to bring his son's body out of the house until the policemen were pulled back from the front door.

Across the street stood about 20 young men who were clearly associated with the IRA. Tensions were high on both sides and trouble could have broken out at any moment. I stood by silently watching the men across the street glaring at the police and listening to the irate father yelling obscenities at the police commander. I could feel the tension in the air like I could feel the rain on my face.

In this super-charged situation, I stood immediately behind the commander and he overheard me when I asked a friend: "When do you think they'll bring out the body?" Upon hearing my American accent, the commander immediately spun around and stabbed his fist hard against my chest and shouted, "Where the fuck are you from in the states?" (He obviously thought I was an American IRA sympathizer who was in Belfast supporting the republicans.) Without thinking, I staggered backward in anger and yelled, "What the fuck do you care?"

In retrospect, it was a dumb thing for me to use that kind of language in such an emotionally-charged situation, but I think my flare of anger reflected my American naivety. I saw myself as a neutral and I had only asked an innocent question. Now, however, I was the object of everyone's attention. Even the young men across the street were looking at me and wondering who I was.

A long silence followed as the commander and I stared at each other. It suddenly occurred to me that I was alone in this country and he was in charge of a large group of police officers who were very tense. After what seemed like a lifetime, the commander turned his back on me and walked away. I remained silent for the rest of the morning and stayed away from the police as the funeral procession moved away from the house. Tension mounted on both sides.

A half-hour later, on command, the police charged the young men who were serving as the honor guard for the dead IRA man. There were a few arrests, but no one was injured. Gerry Adams, President of Sinn Fein (the political arm of the IRA) was right in the middle of the melee. He held back the younger brother of the dead IRA man as the boy tried to attack the police. The boy was only about 10 years old, but it was easy to imagine that he would someday join the republican movement when he was older.

As the funeral progressed through the narrow streets, there was a profound silence. One could feel the anger building on both sides. The expressions on the faces of the bystanders and the police were identical. I do not remember ever being in a situation (before or since) that was so filled with negative emotion. There was a feeling of mutual hatred covering the procession that reminded me of what I called the "Belfast Fog," that I discussed earlier.

For Johnny Coughlin, this was part of the world he experienced every day as he shouldered his 35-pound TV camera on one shoulder while he carried a small step ladder with his other hand. From time to time, he stopped walking and stood on top of the small stepladder so he could film above the heads of the angry folks from both sides. He was extremely vulnerable as people in the crowd bumped against his stepladder.

One day, Johnny's wife, Geraldine, (at home) watched her husband on his precarious perch through the lens of another TV station that was covering the disturbance. She saw a man intentionally push Johnny off the stepladder into a deep ditch along the road. Johnny suffered a broken shoulder and was unable to work while he was recovering.

On another occasion Johnny had put his TV camera away when he was taken prisoner by a loyalist gang during a riot. They must have recognized Johnny's Dublin accent as they dragged him back into an alley by the garbage cans and put a pistol to his head. All this time, Johnny was yelling, "Don't shoot me, I'm a journalist." The man with the gun said he'd never seen Johnny before and was ready to kill him as a probable enemy. Johnny told me that at this point he was face down in the alley, but he suddenly left his body and observed the situation from about 10 feet above. A moment later, another gang member said he had seen Johnny earlier with a TV camera. They took the gun away from his head and told him to "get out of the neighborhood." At this point Johnny returned to his body and ran for his life.

This was the closest brush with death Johnny had, but he continued his work until a ceasefire was called before the power-sharing government was organized after 1998. Since then, Johnny has retired and he and his wife Geraldine spend more time with his daughter who met and married a local man in Oregon. The daughter and her husband now live in Portland.

Johnny visited my college course titled "War and Peace in Northern Ireland" at Portland State University. The two-hour video can be *googled* under my name or "Johnny Coughlin." In a very informative discussion, Johnny does a superb job outlining all the dimensions of the conflict. He would have been an excellent teacher. The video is a splendid way to learn more about both communities in the North.

10. Off the Beaten Track

Sometimes, late in the evening, my Irish Catholic friend John O'Hare would work himself into a state of mind where he would recount spectacular stories about life in Ireland that seemed to be at least half mythological, and the other half a tall tale that most would not believe. For example, he spoke of a "fairy tree" on the motorway between Belfast and Dungannon with a path around the base of the tree where fairies danced when humans were not around. He claimed that no one in the road-construction crew dared cut down the tree to build the motorway for fear of a curse that would follow them to their grave. It is said that anyone who cuts down a fairy tree will never have a "good night's sleep" for the rest of their lives. John said the crew intentionally built the motorway around the tree to avoid the curse.

Later, I traveled that motorway and came back to John with my findings that the road appeared almost straight and did not appear to be rerouted around any tree. John stuck to his story, claiming that I could not see certain things because I was not Irish. On another evening, he told me of seeing a very short man (about three feet tall) walking along in a rural area on the Belfast Road to Derry. John was by himself during that night journey, but he said the "little person," as he called him, turned away quickly from the headlights and ran into the bushes. "They haven't gone away, you know" he quipped with a smile on his face.

After two or three of these stories I would look at John seriously and say, "Do you really believe what you've been telling me?" His classic Irish response was, "No, I don't believe it, but I know it's true." There was often a bit of twilight between John's Irish views and reality. The twinkle in his eyes gave him permission to launch into yarns that just didn't seem possible. He and I had a special relationship that permitted him to tell stories "Outside the Box." John knew I enjoyed them and he had a wonderful opportunity to expand his imagination.

But I soon discovered he was not unique among Belfast folks of both communities. Some of the most respectable friends I had, were fully capable of telling stories that would raise eyebrows in most of Western society. Among them was a Protestant police officer who claimed he had "lived before" as a Catholic in a small town in the South. He knew folks in that village by name – that he couldn't have known from more than 80 years before. Then, there was a Catholic former member of the IRA who had a very detailed religious vision with a dialogue outside of his neighborhood church. These were very "normal" people who had very convincing stories to tell. I never tired of asking folks about their private lives.

Wherever I went I would ask about local folklore. One old man in County Mayo told me he always carried a crust of bread in his pocket for fear that the famine of the 1840s could come back in an instinct. He said there was a curse that could bring immediate starvation unless a person had something to eat. He showed me an old dry piece of bread he had in his coat pocket.

I was always on the lookout for unusual stories. Often it was just a matter of time waiting for the right circumstances to arise. For example, I spent one weekend with the family of one of my students. They lived on a small farm near the southern border. After dinner the woman of the house told me stories of strange events that happened just down the road. As the evening wore on, the man of the household, who had worked hard all day, excused himself to retire for the night. He was hardly out of the room when the woman leaned over and asked me if I had ever heard of "Banshees?" She explained that they were feminine-like spiritual characters who followed some Irish Catholic families for many years, and visited individual members during the night-time hours to warn of a pending death in the family.

The woman said a Banshee came to their home several years ago, before the children were grown. She and her husband were sitting alone one evening reading when they heard a loud "blood-curdling scream right outside the front door." It was unlike any sound they had ever heard. The woman said she could tell that the Banshee was within three or four feet of the door. She and her husband were dumbstruck by the loud cry. Strangely, neither of them was able to speak or move for a full 10 minutes after they heard the wail. They just sat there frozen in their chairs. She said they were struck with a state of fear and disbelief. Finally, both said in unison, "What was that?"

As it turned out, the Banshee's visit foretold the death of the husband's father two days later. The whole incident affected the husband in a very negative way. He has refused to acknowledge the event and has not spoken to anyone about the subject.

During my total of 14 years in Ireland, I tried to explore the unusual things and visit places that were "off the beaten track." I had a friend from Galway who wanted to show me parts of western Ireland. We traveled to County Clare to a region known as the "Burren." Unlike other areas of the country that are green and scenic, there are portions of the Burren that are a rocky plateau area near the west coast and the Cliffs of Moher.

The region has built up quite a reputation in Irish history. It was visited by the notorious Puritan English general Oliver Cromwell, who crisscrossed the island in the mid-17th century, killing Irish Catholics at every opportunity. Local folks repeated the story that Cromwell's army found the Burren's terrain frustrating because there were "no trees to hang a man, no water to drown them, and no dirt to bury them." It has remained to this day an unforgiving part of Ireland.

There were secluded parts of the Burren that reminded me of the face of the moon. I wouldn't think there would be anyone who would choose to live in such isolation. But my friend knew a family that lived in a dark, hollowed-out canyon where the husband tended wild goats. The man of the house also thatched roofs for others who lived a few miles down the road. We had quite a time finding the house. There were no reliable maps showing trails in this remote part of Ireland.

At the beginning of our conversation, the man of the family asked me not to photograph his family or their house. It was a strange request, but I respected their privacy. I remember the whole family had an "other worldly look." They just didn't seem to fit into the Ireland I knew.

There was no electricity in this area, but the family was very generous with their humble resources. In the evening, we dined outside around an open fire on goat meat and goat milk. We sat in the dark and watched the stars move across the sky. These folks spoke a dialect I had never heard before, but I was able to understand most of what was said.

After dinner, the woman of the household told us in a casual way that she had steady contact with spaceships that visited their little domain. She said that "the beings" (as she called them) on the spaceship had a special interest in her goats. She didn't know why, but they took several of the animals on board their ships. They kept the goats, but she and her family felt perfectly safe with their visitors from another world.

The next day we walked a short distance to a cave which our host said was occupied by "little people" who seldom came out of their underground caverns. We started to enter the cave, but I had a strange feeling that I should not follow. I felt fearful about that opening in the ground. The steep entrance was littered with large loose boulders that were wet and slippery. Our host was disappointed that we didn't go into the cave, but I just couldn't explain the negative feelings I had.

So, we left the Burren and went to the nearby village of Lisboonvarna, where once a year, in September, local matchmakers bring in several busloads of marriageable women from eastern Ireland, especially from Dublin, to meet the eligible bachelor farmers from County Clare. As luck would have it, the match-making was in full swing when we were there. My friend and I entered one hall where men were seated on the right side of the room and the women were on the left. There was a country-western band playing, but no one was dancing.

I noticed that the official matchmaker, Willie Daly, was talking to several men who seemed to lack basic dating skills. He apparently was trying to entice the bashful bachelors to walk across the hall to meet the women who were decked out in their Sunday-best dresses. I could only imagine what the match-maker was saying to the men, who looked very uncomfortable.

Later, I found out that folks all over Ireland knew of the match-making in Lisboonvarna. There were stories of lonely farmers in the West who owned land and a cottage. The only thing missing in their lives, was a woman in their humble home. On the other side of the equation were single women from Dublin who saw Lisboonvarna as their last chance to get a husband.

We didn't see any of the bachelors cross the floor, but we heard accounts of how the main matchmaker produced several weddings each year and how he kept the names of the successful couples in his "lucky book." According to local folklore, anyone who touched the book was assured of getting married within six months. One frustrated woman, not only touched the book, she sat on it. I asked about her, but no one seemed to know whether that woman ever got married.

Lisboonvarna was a lively place the day we were there. There were several pubs and hotels where country music was playing all day long. As I sat in one of the pubs. I reflected on the spectacle of matchmaking, screaming Banshees, folks who had "lived before," a famine that could come in instant, an isolated family with wild goats, spaceship stories, the little people who lived in a cave, and the fairy trees. I concluded that this could only happen in a part of Ireland where tourists seldom ventured.

The string of events and reflection on Irish mythology reminded me of my late friend John O'Hare, whose favorite saying was, "I don't believe it, but I know it's true."

11. A Three-Cornered Conflict

I must tell you again how I tried to shield myself from personal danger while in Belfast. I engaged in self-talk in which I declared my identity and purpose in such a way that I would be protected from any negative responses in my environment. When planning to enter a setting that might be dangerous, I would say to myself:

> I am here to learn and understand a situation, so I am entitled to seek information that might not be available otherwise. I am not a participant in this conflict, so I should not be restrained in areas where the public is not welcomed. I have no ulterior motive in my research activities.

Before you read on, let me say I know the above proclamation sounds hopelessly naive. Just saying something like this, does not make it so. But my self-talking did give me a neutral status, and it cleared the deck for me. *I had to establish my credentials in my own mind before I presented them to someone else.* In a strange way, this internal statement authorized me to do things that I would not have done otherwise. I said this kind of thing to myself repeatedly as I squared my shoulders before going out the door every morning. I'm almost embarrassed to put my self-talking in writing, but it was part of my daily routine in Northern Ireland during the Troubles. It was important to me.

I reminded myself that if I just wanted to read about a situation, I could have stayed home and read through someone else's account, but if I wanted to dig deeper, I had to go out on the street to find out what was happening. This has always been my rationale in doing research and teaching. There has never been a substitute for getting out the door and doing it myself.

This was my thinking when I decided that my most important first step in Belfast was to make personal contact with the people who were on the front lines of the conflict. On my first full day in the city, I went to (what I had heard) was the headquarters of the Ulster Defense Association (UDA) the largest Protestant paramilitary group in Northern Ireland. As it turned out, the UDA had a very modest, dingy, unmarked headquarters in East Belfast with a closed-circuit video camera on the outside wall. I knocked on the door several times before a man in camouflaged clothing opened the door a crack. He asked me what I wanted, and I told him my name and said I wanted to come in to talk about the UDA. He shook his head and said "No" and closed the door in my face. I knocked again and another man came to the door. He said the same thing. This time I added that I just wanted to come in for a cup of tea. His response was, "Nobody just comes to our door for a cup of tea," but after I refused to take "no" for an answer, he finally let me in.

The place was a mess, with empty beer bottles and pamphlets scattered over the table and militaristic posters hanging on the wall. It was about 11 o'clock in the morning and there were several men inside, mostly dressed in military-type clothing with tattoos on their arms. They all looked at me with disbelief, asking me again, "Why did you come here? Are you a journalist?" Finally, one of them (who seemed to be in charge) washed out a dirty tea cup in cold water with his fingers, poured a cup of hot water, and offered me a tea bag.

Our conversation was strained from the beginning. He introduced himself as "Joe," and it was three days later that he finally told me his real name was Raymond Smallwoods. Within a few days I discovered that Ray was the major spokesperson for the UDA. It was pure luck on my part that I met him that day. I was full of questions, but on that first morning, he asked me just as many questions about myself. It was the beginning of an unusual friendship that was to continue for several years until Ray was killed by the Irish Republican Army (IRA).

That morning I developed a personal policy even on minor matters – to always tell the *complete truth* when dealing with people who operate in the shadowy world of paramilitary fighters. They will find you out, and it is hard to say what they would do if they caught you in a lie. I soon learned that Belfast really was a small place where people watch strangers (like me) who prowl around their neighborhoods. Days later, Ray told me that people down the street had called them on the telephone that morning to tell them about a man with a beard and a camera around his neck who was walking up the street. (I had the camera so everyone would think I was a noncombatant tourist, meaning no harm to anyone.) Sometimes I took photographs, but the camera was really a prop.

I remember them asking me that day if I knew my way around the neighborhood – in truth they already knew the answer, they were just checking me out. On this same practice, years later, I showed one of the UDA people a chapter from a book I had written on American politics. He said, "Oh I read that long ago, we ordered a copy of that book to see if you were on the up and up."

My relationship with Ray Smallwoods grew into a rather odd friendship that was completely unexpected. He was leery about me from the beginning, but we soon got to know each other better. That first day we talked about an hour at the UDA headquarters before he said he had to leave. I was on foot, so I asked him if he would drop me off in the city center. Before he unlocked his car, he got down on his knees and looked underneath the car, looking for a device that might explode. He explained to me that the IRA used bombs with a mercury-tilt switch that was designed to detonate when the car leaned a bit as it turned the first corner.

During the next week, I discovered that Ray was a marked man. The IRA had tried to kill him several times and they finally would succeed a few years later. But on that first day, I discovered he was also a bit lonely. Ray was very vague at first, but he slowly lifted the veil of secrecy around his personal life. He told me that his youngest son had a learning disability. Ray also admitted that he wasn't the best husband or father-figure in the world. He had served time in prison for attempting to kill Bernadette Devlin who was one of the best-known Irish republicans. I was to find out later that Ray Smallwoods was known most of all for that unsuccessful attempt on Bernadette Devlin's life. Also, I was to learn that my association with Ray would be a problem when dealing with Irish republicans. But on that first day, none of that came up.

There is something about riding together in a car for several miles that causes people to talk. At first, we talked about everything, but nothing of any substance. Later, however, we actually became guarded friends. During the next few months, I met his family, went with him into paramilitary drinking clubs, and accompanied him to the prison to meet his friends who were serving time for paramilitary offenses. We became an unlikely duo, talking about the Troubles, always from a Protestant perspective, even though he didn't believe in God and never went to church.

There were times I had to interrupt him and his friends and remind them not to tell me certain things because I never wanted to hear things I *shouldn't know*. We often met in a pub in Lisburn (just 8 miles from Belfast). Because I was with Ray, I was treated as a friend by everyone. The topic usually turned to current problems within the UDA. Most of it was just idle chatter, but sometime I felt they forgot I was an outsider who might have contacts with the other side.

At the same time, I was building my contacts with the UDA, I was trying to develop relationships with Irish republicans in Catholic West Belfast. Again, I used a direct approach, but it fell flat. People who had an association with the IRA were much more difficult to meet because they were constantly under threat by undercover police officers and British agents who were trying to infiltrate their operations. When I tried to "visit" Sinn Fein headquarters on the Falls Road, I met with complete resistance. There seemed to be no way to get past the front door. My old ploy of wanting to come in for a cup of tea was not even close to being successful. The door keeper had dealt with too many clever pretenders. He offered me no hope of getting through to anyone who would talk with me so I had to try something different.

I knew that the Austin black taxis on the bottom of the Falls Road were associated with the IRA, so I started talking with a man who guided people into the proper taxis that would take them into specific Catholic neighborhoods. Charlie Gilheaney (who died later of natural causes) was a friendly man who obviously knew a lot more than he would say to me. My comments about the weather or Catholic neighborhoods were always met with the same smile and nervous laugh. He never told me anything of importance, but he soon got to know my name, and he seemed to enjoy our conversations. It was clear to me that Charlie must have been trusted by the so called "hard men" within the IRA, in part because he knew how to avoid answering questions while appearing to be friendly and open to a complete stranger.

The first day I met Charlie he suggested that I take a tour of Catholic West Belfast in a black taxi. Not knowing anything about this particular driver, I sat in the front seat and began making conversation. I asked if, by chance, he knew a Belfast Catholic musician named Noel (last name omitted) that I happened to know back home. To my complete surprise he said he had gone to school with Noel and had just been talking to Noel's father that morning. Again, it was dumb luck that "opened the door" through the taxi driver. Within minutes he dropped me off at Noel's parents' home in Catholic West Belfast

Noel's mother and father were delightful. When I told them I knew their son, they invited me inside and later, on that sunny afternoon after we had lunch, we sat out in the back garden and had a few glasses of white wine. On about the third glass, I told them that Noel had told me a story that I didn't really understand. He said his father had always presented a pro-British point of view at the dinner table even though Noel knew his father had "no time for the Brits." Noel didn't offer a reason, but he said, "When you go to Belfast, look up my da and ask him." Noel's father listened carefully to my account from his son.

After hearing the story, he went back inside the house and brought out a single piece of paper that had been folded and unfolded so many times that it looked as though it would fall apart. It was an essay Noel had written years ago when he was in school. The title was, "Why I Know My Parents Love Me." In the essay, Noel said he thought his father had always taken a pro-British point of view because he didn't want to increase the anti-British sentiment in the household. Noel went on to write that his father was trying to discourage his son from joining the IRA. The essay ended on the sentence, "I know my parents love me because they don't want me to "get involved" and end up in an "early grave in Milltown Cemetery."

As I completed my reading, I looked up to see both of the parents with tears streaming down their cheeks. Noel's mother said, "After Noel went to bed each night, we looked through his pockets and found out he was already going to IRA functions." His father added, "We didn't know how else to stop him so we borrowed money to get him out of the country." So that's why Noel ended up in Portland, Oregon.

Later, I recounted that story to Charlie Gilheaney, who showed a wee bit more trust in me as he introduced me to other black taxi drivers who were slowly beginning to tell me about their own lives. It was a very slow and careful process. I applied the same rule I had developed with people in the UDA – always tell the complete truth.

From the beginning, I told the Catholic black taxi drivers that I had con-

tacts in the Protestant community as well. It surprised them at first, but looking back, it was important to be up-front at the beginning because if I were
not, the word would soon be out and other drivers would no longer talk
to me. Also, I found they had a natural curiosity about the folks who lived
across town. After a week or so, they asked me some questions about my
"friends" on the other side.

As I was to find out later, political activists in Belfast kept their eye on a
person (like me) who asked a lot of questions. The taxi drivers were careful
not to make idle comments. I was an unknown character and no one knew
for certain why I was so eager to talk with them.

Just from listening to brief comments, I could tell that all the Catholic
black taxi drivers I contacted had either served time in prison or had some
association with the IRA. But unlike Protestant paramilitary members, these
men played their cards very close to their chests. They were slow to trust a
stranger. It was a very cautious situation. The drivers were courteous, but pur-
posefully distant. I could tell by the expressions on their faces that they were
checking me out. But within a few weeks they began to call me by my first
name as I showed up each day at the bottom of the Falls Road.

I was surprised to learn that if I were introduced by one of them as being
"a friend," others would extend themselves immediately. I soon discovered
that the Catholics of West Belfast were distrustful of strangers generally, but
willing to accept someone who was known by other Irish republicans. As I
met more of them, I discovered they already knew quite a bit about me. They
had been discussing me when I was not around. It was a slow start, but I actually built some close friendships during several years among those who had
learned the hard way not to trust a stranger. In some cases, it took more than
a year before they felt comfortable with me.

One of the drivers, who was also a published playwright, wrote a stage
play about me in which I (as an American professor) became deeply involved
in the Irish Republican Army and a woman who was a double-agent for the
British. It was full of intimate details. It almost made me blush when I discovered the things I could have done in Belfast. But near the end of the play,
I was ambushed and killed by loyalist gunmen. I read the entire script, but I
never showed it to my wife. By comparison, my real life in Belfast was rather
dull.

Eventually I developed tentative friendships with several black taxi drivers on the Falls Road. Looking back, I think they came to trust me because I always told them the complete truth about who I was, and my affiliations with Protestants paramilitaries. It would have been so easy to lie or leave out information about my other contacts in Belfast, but I knew that my long-term success was based on being truthful. I never departed from that self-imposed personal policy.

From the beginning I knew that Irish republicans had been involved in a world where a few idle comments could endanger their own safety. I knew if I told them just part of the truth, they would likely find out what I really had done. They were much more careful with me than the men I had met in the UDA. In the earlier stages of our conversations, I avoided controversial topics when I spoke to my contacts on the Falls Road. We talked a lot about the United States and my life as a college professor in Oregon. Our friendship came first, the conflict in the North came up later.

But both my Protestant and Catholic friends were a bit surprised, and a little suspicious, when I told them I had developed friendships with police officers in the Royal Ulster Constabulary (RUC). At first, my paramilitary friends had facial expressions of disbelief, but they were all very interested. I think they were amazed that contacts of this kind in Belfast could actually occur in an accidental way. I shared the stories with my new acquaintances in the UDA and IRA of how I met with the police.

To begin with, one of my relatives back home was a police officer in southern California. When I told him about my travels to Belfast, he asked if I would trade some police insignias and emblems with officers in Ireland. With these badges and pins in hand, I walked into, what I knew, was the most fortified police stations in all of Belfast. There were sandbags all around the building. The station had been bombed recently. I was carefully frisked at the door. Everyone gave me a strange look. They must have wondered: who was this guy with an American accent who had no business coming into a place where everyone was armed? And why is he talking about trading police memorabilia?

The officer at the desk showed no interest in what I was saying, but my voice is loud, and our conversation was overheard by a police officer in the back room who wanted to see what I had. At the beginning, I felt like a door-to-door salesman placing my police insignias on a table while several officers came out and looked on with interest. I gave away all the badges and insignias I had on that first day with the promise I would get something in return from them next time I dropped by. We soon developed a barter system that was agreeable to everyone. The next time I came in they gave me police emblems I could take back to my relative in southern California. It was a very slow process, but it worked.

Purely by accident, I learned that police officers around the world see themselves as part of an international brotherhood. I met several officers that first day (who were collectors) who became friends of mine during the next few years. I probably was the first and only person that came through the door with "free" police badges from the Escondido, California Police Department.

The end result was that I soon had a small, but eager clientele of police officers who asked for specific items from the United States. I became the go-between-guy for officers from southern California and Belfast. Who would have imagined that arm patches and official hats would become a currency that opened some doors with the defenders of Protestant rule in Northern Ireland?

Each time I came back to Belfast I carried all sorts of bits and pieces of police uniforms that I traded for police articles of every description. It raised many eyebrows with custom officials when I tried to explain why I had all these objects among my personal belongings. One of my prized possessions today is a police whistle that dated back to 1919 when the police across the entire island were called the Royal Irish Constabulary (RIC).

The last year I was in Belfast, one officer gave me a complete RUC uniform. (I had trouble packing the bulky jacket in my suitcase before I returned to the US.) He said he trusted me not to let the uniform fall into the hands of paramilitary members. He jokingly said, "The IRA could cause all kinds of trouble if they got their hands on this uniform."

After a few weeks, several of the officers knew my name and my association with American police officers. They introduced me to other officers who were also collectors of police memorabilia. One officer took me to his home several miles outside of Belfast to show me his entire collection of uniforms, weapons, and documents that proved the authenticity of each item. There were many items from England, Scotland, Australia, and South Africa.

He kept his collection inside a locked room in his home because he said the IRA were known to pose as repairmen so they could get inside someone's home and find out whether they were members of the "security forces." The officer told me that none of his neighbors knew he was a policeman. I found it hard to believe, but he said he never brought his RUC uniform home. According to him, this was common practice among the police, who constantly worried about becoming personal targets of the IRA.

To counter this practice, I found out later that IRA men would park outside RUC stations and follow men home who had probably just taken off their uniforms inside the station. In fact, there was an IRA unit in Belfast that spent a lot of time finding out where police officers and prison warders lived. It turned out that the home addresses were sometimes in error, resulting in some people being killed that were not connected to the security forces.

I had a friend in North Belfast who was shot and paralyzed from the waist down because of mistaken identity as he opened his front door. To make matters worse, his father was inside the livingroom and saw the whole thing and dropped dead from a heart attack. My friend moved out into the country, but his life was forever changed. Sometime later, he and his wife invited me for dinner at their home. I was amazed that he was not embittered by his experiences. Like a lot of folks in Belfast, he adjusted to his new life as a disabled survivor because he had no other choice.

I was surprised by how many folks were eager to tell me their personal stories. One of the RUC men I knew was a police commander. He had about 25 officers in his unit. For some reason, we struck up a friendship. He told me I was the only person he knew that wasn't British or Irish. As our friendship grew, this officer talked about the dangers of being a RUC man in Belfast. I learned a lot about how it felt to be a police officer in a war zone. I didn't ask him questions, he just started talking. Slowly his guard went down as he offered his own point of view of why there was a conflict and how he felt about being caught in the middle.

The last time I saw this RUC commander he told me something he said, he just wanted to "get off his chest." He said his son was a student at Queen's University and had met a Catholic girl in one of his classes. The son brought his new girlfriend home to meet his parents and they had a nice dinner in which they avoided talking about the conflict. The commander said, "I think my son is going to marry her." Then he turned his head away from me and said, "If they have any children, I'm not sure I will be able to love them." He said he was ashamed of what he had just said, but wanted to tell me and see if I thought it was terrible for a man to talk about how he might not love his future grandchildren. At that point I didn't know what to say.

I never mentioned my personal conversations to anyone nor did I reveal the names of any particular officers. The police, like everyone else, were under fire in Belfast. I found it very important to not provide details to anyone else because the information might get back to the wrong people. For example, one of the RUC men confided in me that he had suffered minor seizures because of a head injury. He told me that he would be laid off if his superiors realized that he sometimes forgot where he was, even when he was on duty. The officer has since then retired and he feels much better.

I wonder whether he feels safe now. I've never asked him.

It soon occurred to me that the conflict had three distinct corners: the republicans, the loyalists and the police. All of them were victims in the sense that they felt like they had a target painted on their backs. There were individuals in all three groups who were "marked men." There had been attempts on their lives. One officer told me that his wife had been shot and wounded when she opened the front door to their home. The damage to her face and shoulder was extensive. Other officers said they moved to new houses several times to avoid being targeted by paramilitaries.

In some respects, the police were more isolated than anyone else. They had no natural support group. They were hated by paramilitaries on both sides and disrespected by many regular middle-class people on both sides of the conflict. Being a RUC officer was a dangerous job with few friends outside the police force.

It was a strange relationship I had in Belfast between myself, the loyalists, republicans, and the police. Many things I knew I had to keep to myself. In some respects, *I was three separate people.* As I look back, I can see that knowing certain things made it possible for me to understand comments made by someone on the other side. The fact that I was trusted made me very aware of the special situation I had within these three groups. I would never betray my friends in any one of these camps.

But this three-cornered relationship was very sensitive and could be taken the wrong way if I were seen in public with someone from the other side. The most embarrassing example of this happened one day while I was at the Northern Ireland Parliament building at Stormont in Protestant East Belfast. A media friend of mine introduced me to the RUC Chief Constable. He was a very well-known figure who had testified that day at a legislative hearing inside the building. A local TV crew apparently needed some additional silent film footage so they filmed several minutes of the Chief Constable and I shaking hands and making small talk.

That evening I was with two Protestant friends in a loyalist drinking club. The three of us were sharing a pint and were interrupted by a fourth person who yelled, "Look, Bill's on TV talking to the Chief Constable!" Protestant paramilitary members regarded the RUC Chief as an enemy. I had a hard time convincing everyone that it was a chance meeting and that I did not know the "top cop" in the RUC. My two loyalist friends kept saying, "It sure looks like the two of you know each other pretty well." They commented that the hand-shake "lasted a long time." I don't think I convinced them that I had no connection with the RUC leader. I was reminded again that Belfast is a small place and people notice who you talk to in public.

As I look back at my time in Belfast, I remember that I was on guard nearly all the time. I was always aware of what part of town I was in, and who I knew that lived nearby. Often, I could feel the stress levels rise if I met someone unexpectedly. One particular day I was walking down the street with a Protestant journalist that I met just a few days earlier. As we walked along a downtown street, a well-known Sinn Fein member peddled by on his bicycle and shouted, "Hey Bill, how are you keeping?" The journalist looked at me with surprise and said, "I thought you were neutral on this conflict." He hesitated and then added, "Are you one of them?" I assured him that I was not, but I could feel that he didn't believe me.

There was another chance meeting that caused me real personal embarrassment. A Protestant friend of mine dropped by my apartment for a cup of coffee in the morning at a very inopportune time. It was 15 minutes before a Catholic West Belfast taxi driver was due to come by to pick me up. I was looking at the clock and trying to end the cup of coffee conversation, but I couldn't break off the meeting. We got outside my apartment door, but as we were standing in the street, my Catholic friend pulled up in his taxi. I was mortified and didn't know what to do.

The two men knew of each other because I told both of them about my contacts with the other person, but here they were, meeting for the first time, and I had to introduce them by name. Despite the tension in the air, my Catholic friend (with a smile) reached out his hand. The Protestant man shook his hand, but as he did so, he said very purposely, "So what does the IRA have planned for you today?" I was utterly embarrassed. I didn't know what to say. I just froze and mumbled something about the car was doubled-parked and that we must be going.

As I rode down the street with my Catholic friend, I apologized for the rude remark made by the Protestant man I knew. My Catholic friend just smiled and said, "It's not your fault Bill. They've done worse to me in my life-time. Don't worry about it." But of course, I did worry about it. There were enough hard feelings in Belfast without me causing a new situation full of tension.

But I end this chapter by pointing out that there was one place where sectarian politics didn't come up at all. It was in a really small city center back-alley pub. The bartender there was a member of the Irish Communist Party. He always wanted to talk to me about the Proletariat and the Ruling Class. When he found out I came from Wisconsin, he asked if I would address the local Communists on the Joe McCarthy era in the United States. (The Communist barman knew that Joe McCarthy came from Wisconsin.) I agreed and spent a good deal of time preparing my address. I knew there would be a lot of questions from the floor.

The meeting was held in a large dingy building down by the docks. The air was blue with cigarette smoke. Despite the atmosphere, I was in reasonably good form. I was surprised that the members were so well-versed on recent American history of the Communists Party in the United States. They knew that the US Congress required every Communist to register as an agent of a foreign power. None ever did. They also wanted to know if I had to sign a loyalty oath before I could teach in an American university. I told them that I did sign a loyalty oath and that it still bothered me at a personal level. The 1950s and 60s were a difficult time in American universities.

But here I was speaking to the only group in Belfast that no interest in the sectarian divide. The greatest concern in that hall was the international struggle of workers around the world. Everything was viewed as a world-wide struggle. They saw the "Irish Troubles" as something that distracted people from the "real conflict" with the British and Irish Capitalists.

The Communists were a small, but militant group in Belfast. They even had their own small pub in a city-center alley that I mentioned earlier. That little (hole in the wall tavern) was the unofficial social headquarters for their party. I never encountered anyone there who even mentioned Catholics or Protestants.

After visiting the pub several times, I was always greeted at the door by my man, the main bartender. One evening he announced that I was being inducted into their "Movement" and given a new Irish name: "Comrade Liam O'Meulemans." Every time I went to that pub I was called by my new name. We talked only of the Class Struggle. It never occurred to me to find out whether he had been born a Catholic or a Protestant. But later, I assumed he must have been born a Catholic because "Liam" is a Catholic Irish name.

12. The Hunger Strike

There's an ancient belief in Irish mythology that an individual who has been wronged by persons with authority, through the process of self-denial, can gain a position above those with earthly power. Through the act of refusing food, a single person can rise to a level in society that is higher than any other. On matters of life and death, a hunger strike can become the ultimate weapon of powerless people against their captors.

Dying for the faith was a common practice among early Christians who were tortured and killed by their oppressors. The power of martyrdom was renowned around the world, but it had a special appeal among the Irish who saw it as their means to resist British colonialism. There was something about suffering and self-denial that was very Catholic and very Irish. Offering one's own life was the ultimate weapon when all else failed. It was said that the British had nothing in their vast arsenal to combat a lone Irish soldier who was willing to die for the cause.

Terence McSwiney, an Irish poet and Lord Mayor of Cork, went on a hunger strike inside a British jail in 1920. He is remembered for his view on victory and self-sacrifice. He contended, "It is not those who inflict the most, but those who suffer the most who will conquer." McSwiney died on hunger strike, but his lone battle against his British jailers garnered headlines around the world. His supporters blamed the British for his death. He was victorious as he died inside his prison cell.

The hunger strike for the Irish has always been their tactic of last resort, when all other avenues have been exhausted. And this situation arose for the IRA in 1981 when their cause was in peril. The police had infiltrated the IRA across the province. There was a sharp increase in the number of republicans who were taken prisoner, recruitment was down, and the IRA was losing its momentum. Some were starting to doubt their armed-struggle strategy. Added to this was the public denouncements of British Prime Minister Margaret Thatcher who declared that IRA members were "criminals," that their cause was "a crime," and that they were bound to fail.

At the same time, inside Long Kesh prison, IRA members were struggling to be recognized as prisoners of war. They demanded the right to wear their own clothing, to be free from prison work, to be able to associate with each other, and not to be punished for protesting conditions inside the prison.

British officials refused to recognize the prisoner's demands. There soon developed an impasse, and the IRA began to falter. To counter the downward trend, republican prisoners in Long Kesh went on the offense. First, they wrapped themselves in blankets rather than wearing prison uniforms. Then came the "dirty protest," when they smeared their excrement on the walls of their jail cells. But prison officials also went on the offense, by beating the prisoners and using high-pressured power water hoses to clean out the cells. Then, in a sense of desperation, IRA leaders in the prison considered going on a hunger strike.

There was much debate among republican leaders because the strategy was very risky. The public might not accept the probable loss of human life in a struggle for prison rights. What would happen if the hunger strike failed to attract public support? How would the hunger strike end if IRA demands were not met? There was a lot of doubt.

The first to go on hunger strike in March of 1981 was Bobby Sands, the IRA commander inside Long Kesh who decided to put his own life on the line. The hunger strike became more dramatic when Sands decided to run for a vacant seat in the British House of Commons while in his jail cell. It was a risky move, victory was not assured, but he won in a very close election. Bobby Sands attracted world-wide attention (as a member of Parliament) when he died on hunger strike inside of Long Kesh Prison. More than 100,000 people attended his funeral in Belfast. The story was covered by the press around the world. And like other Irish rebels before him, Bobby Sands was victorious in his death.

After Bobby Sands died, there were nine more republican prisoners who died on hunger strike. When each man died there were riots across the North of Ireland. The world looked on as the hunger strikers became heroes in their own land and around the world. The year 1981 was marked as a time when Irish republicanism turned the corner and regained momentum.

The Irish Catholic Church made an effort to stop the hunger strike on the premise that the men were committing suicide, which was against Church doctrine. Pope John Paul II tried to intercede. He sent a special papal envoy to open negotiations with the British, but London refused to enter talks with the IRA.

I discussed the matter of the Catholic Church and the hunger strike with Monsignor Denis Faul (1932-2006), a local Catholic priest who was very much opposed to the hunger strike. Father Faul told me he had unsuccessfully urged the parents of hunger strikers to take their sons off the strike. In response to his intervention, he said the IRA threatened to kill him if he persisted in his efforts. He told me of a time when three IRA volunteers came to his priest-house in Dungannon and threatened to kill him and bury him in a remote area where he would never be found. Father Faul told me he was proud of the fact that he ignored their threat.

But perhaps the most memorable part of our conversation was Father Faul's admission that, "The IRA beat the Catholic Church at its own game of self-sacrifice." He both praised and criticized the hunger strikers. I found Father Faul was a complicated combination of one who abhorred the loss of life, but who had an open admiration for Irish republicanism. He was an anti-British Irishman to the core who could speak at length about the "atrocities of 800 years of British imperialism," but he was strongly opposed to the hunger strikers fasting to the death.

But unlike the situation with Father Faul, the hunger strike was not complicated for most Irish republicans in the North. The men who died on hunger strike had a following of folks throughout all of Ireland. The memories of those ten men soon moved them into a category at a level with the heroes of the 1916 Easter Rising and others who fought the British during several centuries. The death of each man brought out an emotional reaction from people around Ireland and the world.

Among those who followed the hunger strike was an Irish musician, Brian Warfield, then a member of the Wolf Tones, a quartet of Irish singers that specialized in Irish rebel music. Warfield told me that on the morning July 8, 1981, he heard of the death of Joe McDonnell, the fifth man to die on hunger strike. Warfield said a wave of "historical sadness" came over him. He burst into tears, took the phone off the hook, and sat down and wrote, *The Ballad of Joe McDonnell.*

According to Brian Warfield, it took him just 45 minutes to write an Irish classic that has been sung repeatedly in the presence of Irish republicans around the world. I have been present in clubs behind closed doors where everyone wept quietly as they listened to the ballad. The lyrics are 47 lines long, but just 6 lines from the chorus explain why Irish rebels resented being called terrorists and why they have such a deep resentment of British imperialism:

> *And you dare to call me a terrorist*
> *While you look down your gun*
> *When I think of all the deeds that you have done*
> *You have plundered many nations, divided many lands*
>
> *You have terrorized their peoples, you ruled with an iron hand*
> *And you brought this reign of terror to my land*

Put your reading aside for a few moments. *Google* Brian Warfield on your computer, then add *The Ballad of Joe McDonnell.* First listen to the Wolf Tones sing the entire song while you view scenes from the struggle, and then read the lyrics. There is nothing more to say about why the hunger strike hit such a responsive chord among Irish republicans everywhere.

You may or may not agree, but the Catholics in West Belfast, did prove to themselves that the "British have nothing in their vast arsenal to combat a lone Irish soldier who is willing to die for the cause."

13. Two Friends

The year before I came to Belfast I had been in Israel where I learned there was "always another side to the story." Because of this, I was always looking for someone from the other side to fill in some details that were omitted in the first version I heard. I wasn't long in Belfast before I found myself following the same practice. It might be weeks later, but I nearly always got the chance to hear a very different view of what happened at a particular time.

I soon discovered that there were often three sides to a story: *the Protestant side, the Catholic side, and the truth*. But sometimes the "truth" was interlaced with half-truths from both sides. Often, I would hear an account that suggested one side was completely innocent which convinced me I should search out the other point of view. Hearing the other side nearly always got me closer to what really happened.

My approach to the conflict was always from a comparative perspective. Whenever I found myself "leaning" one way, I would intentionally go out of my way to spend more time with folks on the other side. The result was that I had daily contact with people who had been swept up in events that altered their lives, usually causing pain and personal anguish.

This point was driven home to me one evening after spending the day with people from both communities. It was one of those days in which people had revealed the trials of their lives along with their own personal tragedies. That morning a UDA man had told me how the IRA was destroying Ulster, and why he had a mission to kill members of the republican movement. He also said that he feared he was on the "IRA hit list." He worried about his family's welfare if he were killed. Late that same afternoon, a former IRA man recounted how he had joined the republican movement because loyalists had tried to burn his house down three times. He anguished over his personal philosophy of pacifism while he was a member of a paramilitary army that was involved in organized violence.

When I arrived home that evening, I remember thinking how much these two men had in common, even though they had become mortal enemies. Neither had come from families that had indoctrinated them into sectarian thinking. Both confessed to being rather non-political at an early age.

It was the events around them that propelled them into joining illegal para-military armies. Early in their lives they were attracted to organizations the shaped their future. For the Catholic, it was the Irish Republican Army, and for the Protestant, it was the Ulster Defense Association. Later, they both paid the price by going to prison.

The Catholic man's family had been living in fear because a Protestant mob had tried to set fire to his house while he and his family were asleep. He and another Catholic man took turns staying awake for four-hour intervals to defend their homes. After the third attempt to burn them out, he and his family fled to a safer area. He told me that he joined the republican move-ment because he swore, he would "never be defenseless again."

This particular man had never fired a weapon in anger. Yet he was arrest-ed by the police and sent to prison for having weapons in his home. While in prison the warders told him repeatedly that his wife was going to be arrested, and that his young children would be put up for adoption. Police officers vis-ited his home and told his wife that he "wasn't doing that well in prison." He spent several years in prison where he was housed on a building wing with other IRA members.

Since coming out of prison the Catholic man has avoided additional in-volvement in the republican movement, but despite this return to normal life, loyalists burned out his car just a few yards from his front door. He is no longer an active member of the IRA, but he knows he is being watched by loyalists and by the police. There is nothing he can do except keep his head down.

The Protestant man I mentioned earlier, grew up in a loyalist town where he began to associate with young paramilitary members who convinced him that Ulster was under attack from Catholics who were try to overthrow the state. He became alarmed by the activities of a young republican woman, Bernadette Devlin, who was a leader in the civil rights movement that orig-inated at The Queen's University of Belfast. She was elected as a member of the British Parliament from Northern Ireland and took office on her 22nd birthday, the youngest MP in 50 years. On her first day on the floor of the House of Commons, she slapped a British cabinet member in the face and reportedly said, "This is what you get for murdering unarmed Catholics in

Ireland."

Bernadette Devlin immediately became a target for Protestant paramilitaries in the North. My Protestant friend and two other gunmen were sent by the UDA to kill her in the middle of the night. To their surprise, the police (who had been tipped off) were waiting in the shadows just outside her farmhouse. The police airlifted Bernadette and her husband to a hospital, and thereby saved their lives. The three gunmen were arrested just outside the front door of the farmhouse. They were convicted and sent to prison.

As I reflected on these two men who had become good friends of mine, I came to the conclusion that there were forces beneath the surface in Northern Ireland, that swept them into an eternal conflict without their consent. You may say that they joined the paramilitaries, and therefore did consent. Yet if you knew them and their lives, you would see that events had a way of overtaking individuals – choices were narrowed because of circumstances – minds were made up in the rush of the moment under great pressure.

Many of us would be critical of what these two men did with their lives, but fortunately, most of us will never be confronted by the same desperate circumstances they faced. We will never know what we would have done if faced with those same choices.

These two men underwent a dramatic set of experiences that changed their lives, but my third friend told a story that was very personal, and perhaps more psychologically insidious in nature. I first met Sean in the library, where he told me that, as a child, he watched his father being forced to acknowledge that Catholics, "were inferior because they followed their Church blindly and could not think for themselves."

The story goes that his father was employed as a worker on a large estate outside of Belfast. His job was to tend the horses and clean out the barn where other animals were kept. The so-called "lord of the manor" told a sectarian joke to Sean's father about how house cats were born with their eyes closed, but after a few days their eyes opened. The employer declared that kittens are "born as Catholics with their eyes closed, but when their eyes open, they become Protestants kittens." The employer retold the story many times and laughed as his Catholic workers silently would look down at the ground. He followed up his joke by laughing and reminding his employees that "Catholics followed the Pope blindly, and couldn't think for themselves."

Sean said that, as a boy, he was required to "stand by" and watch his father being repeatedly humiliated. The employer asked his father and the other workers to repeat the phrase, "Only Protestant kittens have their eyes opened." His father was then required to say, "I wish I had been born a Protestant so I could think for myself."

According to Sean, the job included a small house on the estate. His father needed the job and had no other choice but to look down at the ground, and accept the humiliation. He was afraid to disagree because he feared he would be fired. Sean said this was the memory from his childhood that he could not forget – watching his father with his head bowed agreeing with the lord of the manor who controlled his worker's futures and the future of their families. He said he watched his father "put up with the humiliation because he could not find another job to support the family."

14. Mixed Marriages

During the darkest days of the conflict, some individuals who loved each other were afraid to express that love by getting married for fear they would be killed by loyalist paramilitaries. There was an effort to maintain the "purity" of Protestant neighborhoods by eliminating Catholics who married Protestants. In some instances, both of the people in the couple were killed, in other cases, just the Catholic was "taken out."

When I first arrived in Belfast, I lived in a small community of clergy from both sides that counseled persons who were considering a mixed marriage. Prospective couples tried to find a path that would assure them acceptance and safety in the wider communities. Sometimes they could move into middle-class areas in the suburbs, or into Irish nationalist neighborhoods controlled by the IRA. But young people in a mixed marriage were almost universally afraid to live in a Protestant working-class part of town.

Irish republicans did not target a person because of religion or ethnic background, but Catholics did take note of people who had crossed the line to find a spouse. There were some areas considered safer than others, but persons in mixed marriages were nearly always concerned about their own safety. Not crossing the line into a mixed marriage seemed to be the safest practice in all parts of town.

I knew a Catholic man and a Protestant woman who met secretly in a Belfast city-center pub because it was the only place where they didn't think sectarian gangs would see them. They came separately into Belfast from a nearby town after working hours and sat in a back booth away from public view. They overheard my American accent and thought they could trust me because I wasn't involved in paramilitary organizations. To my knowledge, no one else in the pub knew their secret. Some evenings, I would sit down with them, and they would tell me how afraid they were that someone would find out about their relationship and target them to be killed.

It was general knowledge that some Protestant working-class people viewed Catholics in a way that was reminiscent of how right-wing Americans saw Mexicans or Black people. I have been among Protestant paramilitaries in Belfast who referred to Catholics as "Wetbacks" or "Niggers." I recall conversations in which some wondered if these "outcasts" had the same political rights as "normal" people. This kind of speculation made it easier to justify "purifying" the neighborhood by attacking folks that loyalists thought should be eliminated.

I was very sensitive to this situation because two of my close friends of different religions had fallen in love and wanted to marry each other. (I will not use their real names in this story to protect their safety.) Jim was a Protestant man from East Belfast and Kate was a Catholic woman from the South of Ireland. Jim was a community worker in Belfast, and he had met Kate in Dublin at a meeting in the South for community organizers. They had known each other for more than a year and they decided to marry.

Kate said she would be willing to move to Belfast so Jim could keep his job in the North. But Jim knew if he married Kate, they would never be able live in his old East Belfast neighborhood. That area was the home-base for a particular group of zealous Protestant paramilitaries who would never permit a Catholic person to live in their part of the city. Jim also wondered if his mother, Anne, in East Belfast might be ridiculed if her son married a Catholic.

Finally, after a lot of discussions, Kate and Jim decided to take the first step and get married, but not let anyone in Belfast know about their decision. The ceremony would be held in a Catholic church southwest of Dublin. Folks in the South would be invited to the wedding, but friends and family from the North would not be told about the pending marriage. Attendance from Northern Ireland would be limited to the mother and brother of the groom. It was important that no one else in the North would know they were going to be married in a Catholic church.

It was a surprise for me when Jim asked me to be his best man because his only brother, Chris, had taken an oath as a Belfast Orangeman to never enter a Catholic church. Chris said he wanted to attend the dinner the night before the wedding and the reception, but he would remain outside the church building. He promised not to tell any of his friends about the occasion, but his oath as an Orangeman prevented him from ever "darkening the doorway of a Catholic church."

Anne, the mother of the groom, had not taken any oaths of that kind. She was excited about attending her son's wedding and went out and bought two new dresses. I had gotten to know Anne quite well during various family meetings at her home.

It was determined by Jim that I would drive his mother to Dublin the day before the wedding. As we crossed the border, she told me that she had never been to the South and wondered if she would be safe. She told me all sorts of stories about how "clannish" Catholics were. She had heard there was widespread discrimination against Protestants in the South. She was really frightened.

I told her there was no need to be worried, but as we neared Dublin, she began to perspire and had trouble breathing. I realized how untrue sectarian stories could influence a person's sense of safety. When we entered Dublin, she was increasingly afraid. There was nothing I could say that would make her feel safe.

When we arrived at the restaurant for the dinner, I asked Anne if she would wait in the car for a few minutes while I went in to find out if we were at the right place. I met a few of the women inside and told them about the groom's mother out in the car who was nearly paralyzed with fear. I told them that Anne had never met *any* Catholics socially and that she had never crossed the border into the Republic of Ireland. The Catholic women inside the hall all volunteered to help and assured me they would make Anne feel at home.

From my point of view, the next few hours were the high point of the whole weekend. The women in the restaurant went out of their way to welcome Jim's mom. They gathered around Anne and complimented her on her new dress, and exclaimed about how they thought her son Jim was the nicest man they ever knew. The whole atmosphere was exceptionally warm and friendly.

Anne was a practical, down-to-earth, working-class Belfast woman who had never been involved in any festive occasions except Protestant working-class holidays. She was clearly outside her comfort zone, but after about an hour, she came over to me, nudged me in the ribs and whispered, "Ach Bill, they're so nice to me, I'm not afraid anymore." After two glasses of spiked punch, she really looked and acted more relaxed.

When we sat down to dinner, I was told that I was to be the master of ceremonies at the reception that evening. It was news to me, but I found it gave me a chance to speak, not only about the love of Jim and Kate, but also their combined courage to build a marriage across religious lines. I was very careful not to denounce anyone, but I emphasized that love can cross religious boundaries. I didn't have to go into detail because everyone in the room knew that mixed marriages were not common in the North, and they also realized that marriages of this kind didn't occur that often the South either. That's part of the reason why there aren't that many Protestants in the South.

It's doubtful that many in the room knew of the inherent personal dangers of this kind of wedding in the North, but they all seemed to approve of the pending marriage between Kate and Jim. I did notice the priest at the dinner was very quiet. I was told later that he had asked the bride why she "couldn't find a good Catholic man to marry." The priest didn't voice any disapproval that evening, but he didn't go out of his way to be friendly either. He left the reception early without making any comment.

That evening I took a special opportunity as the MC to introduce Anne, the mother of the groom. By this time, everyone in the room knew she was a Protestant who had come down from Belfast for the first time in her life. The word had spread around the hall that she was afraid to be among so many Catholics. I was certain that it was one of the reasons why the applause for her was so long and loud. Everyone in the hall stood up. It was one way that folks in the South could show their acceptance of the groom's mother and their rejection of sectarian rules in the North.

Anne stood and smiled throughout the prolonged clapping. I doubt whether there was a dry eye in the house. I can still see, in my mind's eye, the scores of people who shed a few tears that evening as they welcomed the mother of the groom. Even Chris, the Orangeman brother of the groom, stood and applauded. He wouldn't come into the church the next day, but he recognized his brother was taking a courageous step as he married across the religious boundary.

The actual wedding and the dance that followed went off as planned. Everyone there congratulated the bride and groom, but they showed an almost equal interest in Anne, the groom's mother. There was a recognition that love and affection had won out over sectarianism in at least one part of Ireland that evening.

We all drank more than we should have, and stayed up too late, but when morning came, I was told I should ride back to Belfast with the groom's brother, Chris, who had kept his oath as an Orangeman. He had enjoyed the wedding reception without entering a Catholic church. I remember how odd it looked as Chris stood outside at the bottom of the church steps all by himself. In some respects, it was a symbolic example of the cultural/religious differences between the North and the South.

It was a long 90-mile road back to Belfast and Jim's brother and I talked at length about the Orange Order, its position on the Catholic Church, and the division between the two major religions in the North. Unlike his brother, Chris said he had never "befriended a Catholic" in his life. He insisted that "Roman Catholics" (as he called them) could never be active citizens in a democracy because they were always told what to believe by the local priest. He didn't think Catholics could ever be free as long as they "took orders from Rome." I recall he had a very serious look on his face as he wondered how his brother could ever live with someone who "couldn't think for herself."

As we drove up to Belfast, Chris did most of the talking. I just sat there and interrupted him by saying, "What do you mean by that?" He was thoroughly committed to maintaining the British Union that he credited with all the advances in Ulster prosperity and culture. Again and again, he reminded me that he was "British," that he loved his country, and that he would never "give in to Irish terrorists who refused to obey British rule."

I asked Chris how he felt about his brother after the wedding. At first, he was noncommittal, but then he went on to say he would probably never be close to his brother again. Chris wondered out loud why Jim hadn't looked around more and found a "good Protestant girl to marry."

I knew from personal experience that there were a lot of folks in Ulster like Chris. It was pretty clear that Jim and Kate would have difficulty if they decided to move to Belfast so Jim could keep his job. So, after a time, the newly married couple decided it would be uncomfortable and maybe dangerous for them to live anywhere in the North. Among other things, they considered the problem of raising children in a sectarian atmosphere. Then they would be faced with the question of whether to send them to a Protestant or Catholic school, or perhaps to one of the few independent schools?

It was a tough decision, but Jim and Kate made a permanent move to the South of Ireland. None of their Catholic neighbors seemed to know or care that Jim was brought up as a Protestant. The bride and groom visited Jim's mother in Belfast, but maintained a low profile as a couple while in the North.

I should update the topic of mixed marriages by adding that today, nearly everyone agrees that mixed marriages are occurring more frequently in Northern Ireland, but it will take some time (if ever) before folks will no longer care about their neighbor's religious faith. There is now more tolerance toward people marrying across the divide, but many folks would still have reservations about a member of their family marrying someone from the other community.

This point was brought home to me again concerning another mixed marriage inside a family that were very close friends of mine. Early in our friendship, the mother of the Protestant middle-class family told me, "I have nothing against Catholics, but I know I could never have one as a close friend." A few years later, her son met and proposed marriage to a Catholic woman from Belfast.

The mother and the entire Protestant family decided immediately to accept the young woman as their daughter-in-law. Everyone knew it was to be a mixed marriage, but both sides came together to build an extended family. The wedding took place in a Catholic church in Belfast. The immediate members of the Protestant family were all there, but there was one requirement that was a bit controversial: the groom was obliged to take an oath that all the children in the family would be brought up in the Catholic faith. But despite those restrictions, the bride and groom invited friends and members of both religions.

The wedding went off as planned. It was completely free of any sectarian overtones except for one close Protestant relative of the family who refused to attend the ceremony. Later, the rebellious relative admitted to the groom's father that his oath as an Orangeman had prevented him from entering the Catholic church. The groom's father did not accept the oath as a valid explanation. He told me he lost his temper and declared: "That oath of yours is pure rubbish! You refused to attend my son's wedding. This is *my son* we're talking about. I'll never forget this!"

Maybe it will take a lot more reordering of priorities to break down the walls of sectarianism so people can fall in love and marry a person without regard to religious membership. Time may soften this divisive tradition, but it may not happen in this generation.

15. Black Taxis

At the beginning of the Troubles in 1969, public bus service was discontinued in some Belfast working-class areas because rioters burned all the buses that entered their part of the city. No bus service was a major problem for folks in the upper reaches of the Catholic Falls Road and the Protestant Shankill Road because both areas were several miles from the city center, and families without cars needed some means of transportation. The IRA was first to respond by commissioning a group of automobiles driven by their members on the Falls Road that served as small buses carrying six or seven people each in some comfort. These individual vehicles were permitted free passage through the partisan barricades. Soon after, the UVF followed suit on the Protestant Shankill Road with their own group of makeshift taxis.

From that point on, there were two separate fleets of black Austin taxis (one for each community) operating like small bus companies up and down the Falls and Shankill roads plus other working-class neighborhoods in north Belfast and Derry. The standard fares for these taxis were always a bit lower than regular city buses, and the service was better, because the taxis came up and down the road about every five or ten minutes, and they would stop anywhere along the road. Drivers also offered special services to elderly people and families with baby carriages.

To an outsider, it appeared that the two fleets of black taxis were identical, but it was interesting to note that the black taxis of the loyalist and republican taxis developed separate subcultures when it came to informing the driver when to stop, and how to pay the fare. On the Falls Road, passengers rapped on the glass window behind the driver with a coin when they wanted to stop, and they would pay through the front window after they left the taxi. On the Shankill, passengers verbally asked to be let out at the "next stop," and they paid the driver inside before leaving the taxi. I never heard anyone in Belfast who noted that difference between the two taxi operations.

These two procedures became a permanent way of paying the fares. If a passenger followed the wrong method on either road, it meant he or she was from the "other side." I discovered this difference by making a mistake that caused me some embarrassment. It was on the Shankill Road, and I forgot, for a moment, that I was in a different part of town. When I tapped on the window with a coin, everyone looked at me like I was a foreigner, which of course I was. I remember the woman sitting next to me moved away from me like I had a disease. Since then, I always made it a practice to remember where I was, and how to follow the correct procedures for that part of town.

It is widely known that the taxis were associated with the respective paramilitary groups of each community, and that each driver paid a weekly fee to the IRA on the Falls, or to the UVF on the Shankill. By using these taxis, people were demonstrating some measure of support for the sponsoring organizations. Knowing this, there were folks who would *never* use a black taxi, even with the lower fares and better service, but there are those who *always* used them to support "the cause." On many occasions, I have been in black taxis on both roads when I could watch perspective passengers standing on the curb. Most of the people would get in gladly, but a few would refuse the service and not even make eye contact with the driver as a means of showing their disdain for the particular paramilitary group. In a few cases, it was during heavy rainstorms, and I remember thinking they must really have strong feelings of opposition to the paramilitaries to warrant that behavior. In this case, standing out in the pouring rain was a very prominent "political act" of *not* supporting the local paramilitary army.

One of the unintended spin-offs of the black taxis and public bus competition is that working-class neighborhoods have, to this day, some of the best public transportation choices in the province. In middle-class sections of Belfast and Derry, it is not uncommon to wait thirty or forty minutes for a crowded bus during the morning rush hour. But in working-class sections of both towns, one seldom waited longer that five minutes for a much more comfortable ride at a lower price. The black taxis are here to stay.

In recent years, the IRA has been in firm control of nearly everything on the Falls Road, including the taxi cabs, but the UVF has had some difficulty with taxis on the Shankill. A problem developed because there was a serious dispute between rival Protestant paramilitary factions. The Ulster Defense Association (UDA) was the largest Protestant paramilitary group in the North, and they were dominant on the lower portion of the Shankill Road. It was an uncomfortable situation for folks who supported the UVF to ride through that section of the road.

There had been a serious feud between the UVF and UDA for several years. A fairly large number of families from both groups were forced to leave their homes and relocate into areas controlled by their own paramilitary sub-family. In some respects, it was worse than the old sectarian split between Catholics and Protestants because the dispute often broke up individual families into warring blocs. The quarrel was so divisive in some areas that the children in school were split into UDA and UVF factions. At one school, separate recess times were arranged because UDA children were attacking UVF children on the playground.

Many UVF families were forced to move to the upper Shankill Road, but they had to go down the road (through enemy territory) to get to the city center. The UDA marked their territory on the lower Shankill by painting wall murals that threatened the UVF. The defenseless UVF drivers felt intimidated and refused to drive on the narrow lonely side streets on the lower Shankill because they feared they would be attacked.

Finally, the UVF (of all things) turned to the IRA for help. They asked if their black taxis could use just a few blocks of the lower portion of the Falls that runs parallel to the Shankill to avoid the conflict. To the surprise of nearly everyone, the IRA consented to the UVF request. For several weeks, IRA and UVF taxis shared a short stretch of the lower Falls with no problems from the drivers or the people inside the taxis. But the Catholic youth on the Falls Road found out about it and started throwing rocks at *all* the taxis because they couldn't tell them apart. According to my source, the IRA then apologized to the UVF for not being able to control the children on the Falls Road. The experiment ended on good terms between the two opposing paramilitary groups. The whole incident proved that the two sides could communicate with each other when necessary.

Most people knew that the two black taxi associations on the Shankill and the Falls were clearly identified with the paramilitary organizations that controlled their respective roads. In the eyes of the general public, these drivers (from opposing sides) did not appear to have anything in common, but, in truth, they had very similar backgrounds. Most of them (within their own group) had served time in prison for paramilitary offenses, and many of them had grown up in the same neighborhoods and attended the same schools. They all knew their fellow-drivers, and they seemed to share the same purpose in their particular part of town. There was a lot of banter between the drivers on both roads. They all knew each other and had similar political points of view.

Part of their continuous interaction on each road was based on the fact that they were not just driving their taxis. In reality, the fleet of taxi cabs on both roads were mobile intelligence units for their respective organizations. They were always on the lookout for suspicious people lurking about and undercover members of the Special Branch of the RUC in the vicinity. They developed a series of hand signals that warned each other of possible danger. They were an interesting group of men on both roads. I marveled at how they communicated with each other while on the road.

One of my best friends was a black taxi driver on the Falls Road. I probably learned more from him about the conflict than any other person in Belfast. He personally opposed violence, but he had come to understand that armed resistance was the only way to achieve equality for Irish nationalists in the North. My friend didn't approve of every action taken by the IRA, but he decided that it was absolutely necessary to use lethal force against the authoritarian state in the North. I learned from him why Irish republicans would fight on, no matter the cost to them as individuals. It was quite an education for me.

The two of us talked many hours about how difficult it was to tell the story of Irish republicanism to the outside world. Our plan was that my taxi driver friend would travel to the United States and speak to the news media in Oregon, and also to my students in my college course: "Northern Ireland in Peace and War" at Portland State University. We raised the money for his airline ticket, but because he had served time in prison, it was necessary for him to be approved for travel by a British government representative in Belfast.

According to my good friend, it was a long interview where the discussion centered on how much my friend could contribute to American students in a classroom setting. The British official decided to reject my friend's application to visit the United States, because he said, *"You are a taxi driver and you have no academic background or university degree on this topic."* His final words were, "You have no qualifications to speak about this subject?"

My friend's response was, "I was born and raised in Belfast and lived the conflict every day of my life. My whole life has been about what's happened here. *Those are my qualifications."*

But that wasn't enough! He never did get British approval to travel to the United States.

16. UDA Targets at the University

Politics Professor Adrian Guelke of The Queen's University of Belfast was the target of an attempted assassination during the early morning hours in his south Belfast home. Two gunmen from the UDA (Ulster Defense Association), broke into Guelke's bedroom and shot him in the back as he lay sleeping. Fortunately, his injury was only a flesh wound. The assassination attempt failed when their gun jammed and Guelke's wife screamed. The gunmen ran away, but the UDA announced later that they were responsible for the attempted murder of Adrian Guelke.

It was not clear why the UDA would try to kill a university professor who was a 44-year-old White man who had been born and educated in South Africa. Since coming to Ireland, he had not been involved in any Irish or British political affairs that might interest the pro-British, loyalist paramilitaries. He was a professor of comparative politics and international studies that would not have any direct application to sectarian Ulster politics.

A week after the attempted assassination, I dropped by to visit my friend, Adrian, who by this time, was back in his office at Queen's University. My first question was why did the UDA target him? What reason would they have to kill him? Adrian had no idea. He was not involved in local politics. When he lived in South Africa, he had been involved in the Anti-Apartheid movement that opposed segregation policies in South Africa, but he had avoided any involvement in northern Irish politics.

Adrian Guelke's major concern was whether he was still a UDA target? Would they come back and try to kill him again? He had no idea why they were after him. His Irish wife had been born in Belfast, but she was no longer a practicing member of any church. She was fearful that her past religious identity may have something to do with the attempted murder. Adrian was confused and afraid. He just wanted to contact the UDA and find out why they wanted to kill him, but he didn't know who he could talk to that might have ties to the illegal paramilitary organization.

At this time, I had been in Belfast for only a few years, but I had already developed a working relationship with Raymond (Ray) Smallwoods, who was the major spokesperson for the UDA. Ray had been the first paramilitary member I had met in Belfast. Most of our time together was spent on political topics, but there was a personal side as well. I went to his home several times and met his wife and two sons. He told me about his time in prison for an attempted murder. He also introduced me to other members of the UDA who told me more than I ever expected about their illegal organization. At least one-half of all the loyalists I knew were through Ray Smallwoods.

I decided to contact Ray to see if he knew anything about the attempt on Adrian's life. This was the first time I asked him for specific information involving paramilitary activities. I told him at the outset that Adrian Guelke and I were friends and colleagues in the same department at Queens, and that he wanted to know why the UDA had tried to kill him.

Ray was very noncommittal upon hearing my request. He said it was unclear whether he could uncover anything about the motive for shooting Adrian. He was careful with his words, saying he would talk with some other members about the attempted killing, but there was no promise he would be able to tell me anything.

Three days later, Ray and I met in a loyalist pub in another town about 10 miles from Belfast. His opening comment caught my attention. He said he had "good news" for Adrian Guelke, but "bad news" for me. Ray said the UDA had "intelligence" that a "foreign-born faculty member" in the University Politics Department was "an asset of the IRA." The UDA had not been given any names, but the first person they thought of was Adrian Guelke, who, of course, had been born and raised in South Africa. Ray concluded by saying that the whole "operation had been a huge mistake," that Adrian Guelke was no longer a target. He said I could assure Adrian that he was no longer in any danger of being shot by the UDA.

But next came "the bad news," a complete surprise to me.

The UDA was now certain that Guelke wasn't associated with the IRA, but they now believed that there was still "truth" in their intelligence about someone else from a foreign country. Ray lowered his voice and looked me straight in the eye as he said, *"You are the only other member of the Politics Department who was foreign born."* It took me a moment to understand what he was saying. Was I now under suspicion because I was the only other foreign-born faculty member? Ray had a strange smile on his face as he said, "Some of the guys were wondering why you were asking so many questions."

I could feel the flush on my face; I must have turned beet red. For a moment I was speechless. Was I really a suspect? Were all my questions interpreted to be the work of a spy who was reporting to the other side? Ray knew a lot about me. He was fully aware of my research contacts with Irish republicans who were affiliated with the IRA. His next comment was, "Bill, are you trying to walk on both sides of the street? That's "a bit risky, isn't it?"

From my perspective, I was trying to learn about both side of the conflict, but now Ray was suggesting that I had an ulterior motive – that I may have been an undercover agent for the IRA. The first thing I thought of was how could I prove that I was not working for Irish republicans? How could I prove a negative? How could I prove I was not an undercover agent?

There was silence for several minutes. I was staring into a glass of beer, not knowing what to say. Ray was looking at me in a different way. I could tell he was unsure of what to think about me. I felt I could read his mind: "Was I really just an American professor who had an honest reason to ask all those questions, or was I something else?" Perhaps he thought I had developed our friendship just so I could pass information back to the IRA. For the first time in Belfast, I felt real concern for my own welfare.

Ray finally broke the silence. First, he said I should not share any of this with anyone else. Secondly, he said there were still some questions he had about the source of the UDA "intelligence" from South Africa. He said he "smelled a rat," that maybe there was more to the story. He would let me know what he had found.

It was nearly a week before Ray got back to me. I must confess it was a difficult time for me as I considered what I should do. How could I clear my name? Should I break my academic contract with Queens and leave Northern Ireland? Should I try to get the next flight back home? Would that kind of action be interrupted as a proof of guilt? If I tried to leave Belfast, would the UDA come after me? I wasn't sure about anything.

During the next week, I became obsessed as I thought about all the ways someone could get to me while I was sleeping. I knew they could get to me pretty easily if they really wanted to break down the door. I was not armed, and I didn't live in a secure location. For a couple of days, I could feel like a lot of other Belfast folks must have felt who were 'involved" in the conflict. For the first time in my life, I felt personally threatened. I couldn't wait to contact Ray and find out any new information. When I called him on the telephone, he laughed a bit when I asked if there was any news. We got together that evening.

Ray started our meeting by saying he had "good news" for me. He said that a guy named Leon Flores was an agent of the SADF (South African Defense Force), and that Flores had tried to "set up" the UDA to kill Adrian Guelke as a "final retribution" for Guelke's past activities in opposition to the Apartheid policies in South Africa. Ray wasn't sure what Guelke had done in South Africa, but it must have been important. Adrian had left South Africa in a hurry, but they had followed him to Belfast. Apparently the SADF had tried to get Adrian before and failed. This time the SADF agent had actually planned the whole operation by conning the UDA into thinking that Adrian Guelke was working for the IRA.

Ray was a bit embarrassed about revealing the attempted con job because it reflected badly on the UDA. He said that it was a local operation authorized only by the South Belfast UDA, and that other members in Belfast knew nothing about what he termed their "huge mistake."

After the Adrian Guelke matter was cleared up, I discovered that Ray was also playing both sides of the street. He was secretly involved in meeting with two Catholic priests who had ties to the IRA (Fathers Gerry Reynolds and Alex Reid). On the one hand, he was one of the leaders of a paramilitary organization, but he also was exploring terms that might bring a ceasefire to the conflict. But his peace-making efforts would not save him from being a victim of the conflict just a short time later.

I'm certain that the IRA didn't see Ray Smallwoods as someone who was promoting peace. I had heard earlier from several republican sources that Ray was an IRA target. In fact, I was warned that it was "dangerous" to hang around with him. I remember that Ray, at this time, would always sit in a location where he could keep an eye on any outside door. He no longer smiled very much. Looking back, it seemed that Ray had a premonition of what was to come. For some reason I did not take the warning signs seriously. I found out later that the IRA had a list of loyalists they wanted to kill before the republicans declared a ceasefire, and that Ray was on the list.

During the late afternoon hours of July 10, 1994, three members of the IRA took over the house across the street from Ray Smallwood's home in

Lisburn, Northern Ireland. The plan was to kill Ray early the next day as he left his house across the street. But plans changed when Ray left earlier than anticipated. He drove several blocks away from home before remembering that he was scheduled to do a TV interview that morning. He needed to return home quickly and get a sport jacket suitable for the interview. Ray left the engine running in his car as he quickly ran into the house to get his coat. When he returned to his car there were three IRA men with 12-gauge shotguns waiting for him. They caught him in a crossfire. He was killed instantly in his own front yard.

Ray's wife and son watched the entire assassination through their living room window and told me all the details. Ray's wife, Linda, was distraught after the funeral and wondered what she could do to avenge the killing. She had contacted a psychic to see if she could find out the names of the three men who killed Ray. She reached in her purse and brought out a piece of paper and started to hand it to me. I told Linda that I didn't want to see the names, and that she should destroy the paper and not tell anyone else about the information. She followed through that day and burned the paper containing the names of the three possible assassins.

That was the last time that I would see Linda, but I have thought of her many times as another widow of the conflict. My hope is that none of her sons decided to pick up the mantel to retaliate against those men that killed their father.

17. Getting Through the Door

I learned early in life that it was possible to enter a place where I didn't belong if I acted like I had a right to be there. As a child, I found that I could get into a movie theater with no ticket if I said something like, "The person at the ticket counter told me it was all right if I went in to look for my brother." It was important to appear like I was authorized so no one would challenge my entry into the theater. Body posture and the quality of my voice played a large part in "Getting Through the Door." It was really an acting job that took a little courage, but it was a game that was relatively safe to play. Even if I failed to get through the door, the worst I could expect was a short lecture about playing by the rules.

There were many places in the North that were closed to the public. Political parties had confidential meetings where members could speak without fear of being quoted by the press. Political/religious fraternal organizations had private assemblies so they could vent anger against their opponents and stir up their members to a fever pitch. Paramilitary organizations held secret sessions behind closed doors to direct their members on military missions. And even universities had the right to hold an exclusive meeting of all their past graduates to decide a change in policy.

My first effort was a matter of luck. The Ulster Unionist Party (UUP) had difficulty negotiating with Irish nationalists without appearing to be overly friendly. There were UUP members who turned on each other just because one of them shook hands with a Catholic leader on TV or acted in a civil manner at a public meeting. The UUP scheduled a meeting at the Waterfront Hall to let rank-and-file members criticize the leadership without the press writing down every word.

I wanted to get into the meeting, but every door was manned by a uniformed member of the Royal Ulster Constabulary (RUC) who turned away anyone like me who did not have a membership tag. I checked out three doors and I was unable to talk my way into the hall.

But by a stroke of luck, the fourth door was guarded by a police officer I knew well from my trading of police memorabilia between US and Belfast officers. The RUC man and I engaged in small talk as we stood by the door.

Then he said in a joking manner, "If I let you in, and you get caught, will you promise not to tell anyone how you got in?" I agreed and he opened the door a crack while I squeezed through.

It was an intense meeting as members spoke candidly to each other about how to deal with Catholics successfully while not appearing to be too cooperative. One leader was criticized because he smiled while speaking with an Irish nationalist. Another wondered if they could work through the peace process without meeting or talking with the other side. There was a lot of name-calling as they traded verbal jabs back and forth. I learned a lot about their personal views.

I was slouched down in my seat, trying to hide, when one of my university students came up and called me by name. He said "What are you doing in here? You're not even from this country. You have to leave." I nodded my head and said how happy I was to have him as a student in my university class. I think he got my message. I stayed in my seat.

But there was another time I got into a private session that gave me a few anxious moments. I was going to meet with an Irish republican friend in Dungannon which is about 40 miles west of Belfast. It was on a Sunday evening in late November when I phoned him and found he was not at home. His wife (who I knew well) answered the phone and told me where he was. She gave me very detailed directions on how to find him.

I was to go to a local school In Dungannon. She said the building would be dark, but I should go to the door off the playground and let myself in, walk down a dimly-lit hallway to a double-door on my left. She said I should just open the door and I would probably find her husband in a meeting. She didn't say what kind of a meeting it was. I think she thought I realized what kinds of people would be there. It turned out she was wrong.

I followed her instructions walking through the dark building where there were only a few lights marking the exits. I opened the double-door and walked into a room where there was a group of about 20 young men that jumped up from their chairs. Several of them moved quickly toward me in an aggressive manner. They stopped only when my republican friend called me by name and asked them to sit down.

At first, I didn't know what to do. I realized immediately that I didn't belong in this meeting. Everyone looked at me with contempt in their eyes.

My friend (who was chairing the session) quickly called me by name to assure everyone that I wasn't a threat. Without hesitation, my friend announced that the meeting was over. I made a point to *not make eye contact* with any of the young men who walked past me out of the room. My friend said he was glad to see me, but it was clear he didn't expect me to walk into what was clearly a local meeting of the Irish Republican Army. After everyone else left, we walked out of the school basement and went downtown to finish our evening in an Irish pub. We never talked again about the meeting at the school.

As I stated earlier, I was interested to get into meetings of both sides. A special interest of mine had always been the Orange Order which boasted that their membership included about one-third of the Protestants men in the province. Throughout the year they were very visible as they marched through some communities in Northern Ireland. Most of their marches were peaceful, but each year they insisted on marching through a few Catholic neighborhoods that had previously had a Protestant majority. Irish republicans tried to block the Orange marches, but the RUC often stepped in to escort the Orangemen down a street while angry Catholics yelled obscenities at the marchers. Many Orange parades were really a controversial attempt to reclaim lost territory.

Most Orangemen on parade were dressed in their Sunday-best black suits, white gloves, bowler hats, and most noticeable an orange-colored sash around their shoulders. They all looked very serious as they carried the British flag and kept in step with the music played by their flute bands. They often intentionally irritated Catholic nationalists by marching past Catholic churches singing sectarian songs. One of their favorite songs had a phrase of being "up to our knees in Fenian blood." Protestant Orangemen I knew insisted that their parades were completely innocent. Catholics strongly disagreed.

One day I watched Orange marchers stop in front of Saint Patrick's Catholic church on Carrick Hill near the city center. Most of the marchers stayed in the street watching as a few of them broke ranks and walked over and urinated on the front steps of the church. A small number of RUC officers stood by and watched. The whole act took less than ten minutes and the marchers continued their parade into the city center. The next day there were pictures circulating in the pubs of the Orangemen "relieving themselves" on the front steps of the church.

I have attended many outdoor Orange rallies and marches, but perhaps the most interesting was inside Belfast's Ulster Hall. More than 1,400 Orangemen gathered for their annual meeting inside the hall. The Orange sash was a required piece of clothing worn by everyone who was permitted inside the hall. I was stopped by two husky doormen who asked why I didn't have a sash. I mumbled something about how I had forgotten it. But they showed no mercy, especially when they heard my American accent. They grabbed me by both arms and ushered me outside the hall. At this point, I didn't know what to do.

I went around the back of the Ulster Hall and encountered an Orangeman I knew who was standing in line to get in the back door of the hall. He was carrying two cardboard boxes full of song books. I offered to help him and I carried in one of the boxes high enough so no one would notice I didn't have a sash. Once I got inside, I gave the box back to my Orange friend, who never realized why I offered to carry it through the door. As far as I know, I was the only non-member in the hall. I hurried through the crowd so I could get a good seat.

The annual Orange meeting was filled with symbols of God, Orangeism, and the British Union. There were flags and banners everywhere. Once inside, no one seemed to notice I didn't have a sash around my shoulders. I didn't say a word while several members slapped me on the back in a gay, festive atmosphere. They were so happy to be among their "own kind."

After a half-hour of frivolity, the program began. I got a seat near the front of the hall. Speaker after speaker rose to proclaim that there was no man-made law that could bar Orangemen from expressing their Christian heritage by marching where they pleased. The strength of the speakers and the thundering applause was a testament to their marching commitment, regardless of Catholic opposition. But the loudest cheer of the evening was given to a speaker who said, "No one should ever call me an Irishman, because all Irishmen are savages who practice a godless religion." The crowd went wild as he touched on the real reason why Orangemen have such a strong determination to march through Catholic neighborhoods.

A few weeks after the Ulster Hall meeting, I was faced with another challenge of how to get into a meeting of *all the graduates* of The Queen's University of Belfast. The question to be decided by the graduates was whether to continue playing *God Save the Queen* at the beginning of the Queen's graduation ceremonies each year.

This was a controversial issue because a growing number in the recent graduating classes were Catholics who refused to stand when *God Save the Queen* was played. Catholics insisted "She's not my Queen." Protestants, of course, reminded everyone, "If they go to *our* university, supported by *our* tax money, the least they can do is show respect for *our* Queen."

The issue arose when the university faculty senate tried to ease tensions by voting to discontinue playing *God Save the Queen,* and substituting the European national anthem *Ode to Joy* in its place. Protestants throughout Northern Ireland were angry and talked of ways to reinstate their national anthem.

The first ever meeting of *all* the graduates of The Queen's University of Belfast was held on a sunny Sunday afternoon in a large campus auditorium. Security was tighter than I expected. There were tables set up at the entrance for graduates to register before they could enter the hall. Individual graduates were required to go to the appropriate table (by graduation date) and have their names checked off and then be authorized to enter the university hall.

There were scores of graduates standing outside in small groups. I decided to blend in with four men about my age and follow them to the table to be checked off. I stood in close as each of them stated their names and year of graduation. I smiled as I commented to one of them, "It's good to see you again." He looked at me with disbelief because, of course, we had never met each other before. Then the five of us walked into the hall together. Once I was inside, I quickly broke off from the group and went upstairs to the front row in the balcony overlooking the stage.

It was a great seat where I could look down and see the faces of nearly everyone in the hall. Individuals in the audience rose to speak on the question of which music to play during the graduation ceremonies. I did not see one person in the hall who did not either cheer or boo each speaker depending on which side they favored. A well-known member of the Belfast City Council was seated right behind me. His comments to his wife reflected his deep-seated hatred for the other side. The only issue was which music to play at the university graduation.

It's often said that sectarianism is found mostly among working-class people; however, it is important to remember that everyone in that hall (except me) was a graduate of the university and therefore much less likely to be working class in their origin. I think of that point every time I hear folks say that it was just a war between the working-class people on each side. In truth, sectarianism runs deep in all parts of society.

Because there was a Protestant majority that afternoon, the vote was to reinstate the playing of *God Save the Queen* at graduation ceremonies, but the university senate stood by its earlier decision to play the European national anthem, *Ode to Joy*. The final policy on which music to play was not changed, but it did provide a lot of graduates with an opportunity to vent their sectarian emotions.

There was another incident of me "getting through an official procedure" and getting "special treatment" that was quite different. One evening I was introduced to a man who worked for the all-Ireland transit authority. His job was to issue free passes to Irish senior citizens to use all the buses, trains, and ferries for all of Ireland, North and South. It was clear that the passes were meant for Irish citizens, but I wondered if, by chance, I could get a pass.

I told him I could certainly use that kind of pass because I was spending quite a bit of money each year for my travels inside the North and throughout the entire country. He didn't really respond to my inquiry until he asked if I had any political campaign material that he could have. I said I didn't have any with me, but I certainly could bring some back next year.

At this point he took out the application form for the free transportation pass and asked me to fill in my name and Belfast address. He said I needed to prove I was 60 years old and the only proof I had was my Oregon driver's license. He wrote down the number from my license and tucked away the application in his pocket. I received the pass a few days later in the mail and I used it every day for the next eight years. I traveled not only around the North, but I took several trips to Dublin, Cork and Galway. I saved a lot of money and didn't ask any questions.

The next year I brought back several campaign badges and banners from American political campaigns. The man who worked for the transit authority was bipartisan in his tastes. All the buttons and pins had an equal value for him. Each year I brought back more political memorabilia, and each year my civil servant friend would add them to his collection. My pass was renewed several times while I was in Ireland so I had no complaints.

In the process of bringing back American campaign materials I discovered there was a woman working in a local library who had a "crush" on President Bill Clinton. She not only wanted buttons, but pictures and letters on his campaign headquarters letterhead. In return, I was the only one I knew of who had the privilege of checking out videos from the library collection and taking them home for viewing.

She decorated the wall around her desk in the political section of the library with large colored pictures of Bill Clinton. It was impossible to visit the library and not notice the display of Clinton materials plastered all over the wall. It brightened up a dark corner of the library where all old printed records and news videos of the Northern Ireland conflict were kept.

One day she was visited by the Reverend Ian Paisley who had a reputation for being very gruff, formal and serious. He was visibly troubled by the Clinton display and he reminded her that the library was supposed to be "non-partisan." She looked up from her desk and said very frankly, "Dr. Paisley, these materials have nothing to do with politics, it's all about sex."

The Clinton material stayed up on the wall.

18. The Trappist Monk and the Irish Prize Fighter

During my time in Ireland, I discovered there were two people I knew independently that had not seen each other for more than 50 years. One was an elderly Catholic Trappist monk living in a cloistered abbey in Lafayette Oregon, and the other was an over-the-hill, retired Irish Protestant prize fighter living in Belfast. They were an unlikely duo that demonstrated that an old friendship could give both men a new lease on life, and a second chance to shake off their past religious division. It all began as a result of my visit to a remote monastery nestled in the hills of northwestern Oregon.

My wife enjoyed going to the Trappist Abbey in Lafayette, Oregon for early morning services. She told me about an Irish Trappist monk at the abbey named Michael Farrelly who had worked and lived in Belfast during World War II. I went to the Abbey and it wasn't long before Michael and I became close friends. I visited him regularly at the Abbey every Sunday afternoon when I was at home in Oregon. We talked about our own lives, Irish politics, history, and sports over a period of 19 years. We became best friends.

Michael had been born in the South of Ireland. He did not become a Trappist monk until after he arrived in the United States. During World War II he had worked in Belfast doing bomb repair work around the shipyards and other strategic areas important to the British War effort. He and I had long conversations about what Belfast was like during the 1940s, and how the working-class neighborhoods were more relaxed during the War years.

Michael's memories of Belfast were colorful and full of examples of how well Protestants and Catholics got along during the War. Despite the fact that Michael was Catholic, he rented a room in a Protestant household in North Belfast where he developed friendships with young men his age from both religious traditions. Michael's best friend at that time was a Protestant named Billy Reid, whose family owned the rooming house.

Together they toured many of the drinking clubs in the neighborhood and enjoyed the life of young single men in Belfast. They were known around North Belfast for being very good dart players. Michael boasted that he and Billy bet on their ability to shoot darts, and that they seldom had to buy their own beer in neighborhood pubs.

During the War, Ulster was an important industrial contributor to the British War effort, so Belfast had become a target for German warplanes during the War. According to Michael, he and Billy had a great time roaming around the city during the German bombing raids. Everyone else was crouched inside the bomb shelters during the air raids except for them. He said it was just like the movies with the sirens blowing and the roar of German bombers overhead. During the night raids, it was even more exciting because there were search lights. Michael said Belfast was a lively town during the war. He said there was little if any sectarianism until after the War ended.

When there was no more bomb repair work, Michael left Belfast. He spent three months in England, and then emigrated to Canada. A few years later, he crossed the border into the United States. He told me he thought of Billy Reid many times and wondered if he was still in Belfast. Hearing of his curiosity, I decided it would be interesting to set up a situation where these two old friends could be in contact once again.

The next time I went back to Belfast, I went to Dunmore Drive in the Fort William neighborhood where Michael and Billy had lived more than 50 years before. The windows of the old house where they had lived were boarded up and the neighbors told me the house was going to be demolished soon. I spent a good deal of time talking to the neighbors to see it they knew where Billy Reid might be. Folks across the street remembered Billy, but they had no idea where he might be now. One person down the street thought Billy had taken a job as a bread truck driver, but I checked the bakery and found that all their records of their employees had been destroyed in a fire. I discovered in the telephone book that there had been two men by that name in Belfast. I called both of them and found that neither of them had ever lived on Dunmore Drive.

I had almost given up finding Billy Reid when I contacted one of my loyalist paramilitary friends who boasted he could find anyone in the city. I gave him all the information I had, and two days later, he came back with the address of Billy Reid, who he said was partially disabled, and living with his former wife and daughter. He cautioned me to approach Billy carefully and not to say anything that might alarm him. According to my loyalist friend, Billy had a police record and might not be very cooperative in dealing with a stranger.

When I knocked on the door, Billy's daughter greeted me. I told her who I was and why I was there. It turned out Billy was listening around the corner and heard everything I said. He put out his hand and said he was 'happy" to meet me. For the next hour, Billy told me his life's story after World War II. His main job had been driving a bakery delivery truck in Belfast, but he also had joined a boxing club and had several professional fights in Northern Ireland and England. Billy won most of his fights and decided to emigrate to Australia where he heard there would be more opportunities to box and have a better life.

But things didn't go well in Australia. He didn't want to go into details, but from what I could tell, it sounded like Billy bet a large sum against himself in a boxing match, and then lost the bout on purpose. He was embarrassed to tell the story, but he said the authorities found out about him "taking a dive" and put him on a plane and told him he could never return to Australia.

Billy then came back to Belfast in 1983, but his life continued to go downhill. His police record from Australia and his poor health prevented him from getting a steady job. He was suffering from emphysema and had trouble getting around. Finally, Billy moved in with his former wife and daughter who felt sorry for him.

Without any questions from me, Billy spoke extensively about the tensions between the two communities in Belfast. He had spent nearly all of his time with Protestants, but he said he had come to know several Catholics that he respected. He said there were a few Catholics that had come to his aid in Belfast. One of them even helped him get home one night after he had been robbed in a shady part of town.

Several times in the conversation, Billy asked about Michael. Apparently, their friendship was more extensive than I suspected. It suddenly occurred to me that I could link the two of them up by telephone. It was almost 6 pm in Belfast when I decided to call Michael in Oregon. The time at the Trappist Abbey would have been nearly 10 am, and I knew the telephone number that Michael would answer.

Michael knew I was in Belfast, but he had no idea why I was calling. I asked if he was sitting down and then I gave the phone to Billy who said with a strong Belfast accent, "Michael, what about ya? Do you know who this is?" I couldn't hear Michael's response, but Billy nearly dropped the phone. Billy had tears in his eyes immediately as he turned to me and exclaimed, "He called me Buddy. No one else ever called me by that name."

Billy quickly asked, "Why did you become a Trappist monk? You used to like drinking beer." Billy then turned to me and said that Michael "still likes to drink beer whenever he can get away with it." The two of them talked for a long time as they traded memories. I could only hear one side of the conversation, but I knew it consisted of their times in Belfast during the air raids and throwing darts in neighborhood beer halls. Again and again, Billy said, "Do you remember when we ...?" They really enjoyed getting back together after more than 50 years.

That day in Belfast, we turned the clock back 54 years as old friends got together again. They went on for nearly an hour, renewing all their old times at the local pubs.

Before I left Billy that day, I promised I would return later to do a cassette-tape interview with him that I would give to Michael when I returned to Oregon. I assured Billy that I would do a similar interview with Michael that I would bring back to Belfast for him the next year.

I told my friends in Belfast about these two old friends getting together. Without exception, both the Catholics and Protestants exclaimed that it was a "good example of what Belfast people are really like." My northern Irish drinking buddies loved to tell stories about the common people in both communities welcoming outsiders and accepting people of other cultures. It may be a side of Belfast that few outsiders ever get to appreciate.

When I returned to see Billy again one week later, it was clear he had given more thought to the whole experience. He told me he had made a lot of mistakes in his life, but that the phone call gave him a chance to go back and relive the "best days" of his life and remember what it was like to be free of sectarianism. He confessed to remaining silent during many years when he heard anti-Catholics stories. But he said he was always a bit ashamed that he didn't object to the many hateful comments he had heard during his life.

Billy was still in that reflective mood when I turned on the tape recorder. He began by saying, "Michael, you were the best friend I ever had, and I want to thank you for those few years we had together." Billy went on for 90 minutes talking about their times in Belfast and Billy's career as a boxer and truck driver.

A few months later in Oregon, I played Billy's tape for Michael. Neither of us had a dry eye as we listened to the interview. Michael said that he thought Billy had gone through a real transformation whereby he had confronted and rejected the long sectarian patterns of his life. It was like he was voluntarily starting a new life. As Michael listened to the tape, I could see he was imagining himself back in Belfast during World War II. We shared another box of Kleenex.

One week later, I recorded the interview with Michael that I would take back to Belfast. Michael confessed that he also had taken sides in the sectarian dispute in the North of Ireland. He spoke about things he learned in life that weren't related to his religion. There were several secular details I hadn't heard before. He recounted his time as a bartender in Chicago, his move to Arizona and California, and finally the events leading him to Oregon and taking the oath as a Trappist monk in 1955. There was a lot of emotion in his tape, as well. Michael had a far-off look in his eyes as he spoke into the microphone. He told me later that he had never tried before to recount his life over that 50-year period. It was a very reflective time for him.

A few months later, I returned to Belfast. Soon after I arrived, I went to Billy's house with Michael's tape. Billy's daughter met me at the door to tell me that Billy had died the month before of emphysema. But she said that the whole experience with Michael had given Billy a new outlook on life that helped boost his self-esteem. She didn't give many details, but apparently Billy had many low points in his life. She said the telephone call with Michael had caused Billy to become more positive about his entire life. She said he was eagerly awaiting to hear the tape I was bringing back to Belfast. I gave the tape to Billy's daughter so she could relive the memories that were meant for her father.

My experience with Michael and Billy gave me something that was unexpected. There was something precious about seeing two 84-year-old men shedding tears of joy that gave me a different insight to the sectarian conflict in Belfast. It demonstrated that the communal hatred was sometimes just a surface factor. In most cases, there was *another person underneath* that could bridge the gap between the two communities.

I found that sharing fond memories from the past is good medicine in any country of the world. As it turned out, this was especially true about Belfast. Maybe even the "hard men," as they were called, had another side that was more open than we expected. I learned a couple of things from this experience that changed my life.

First, I am certain that friendship reunions can be enormously beneficial to the mental health of all of us. There should be a chance for all of us to celebrate "old times" together. In these circumstances, memories tend to be *gentle*, as folks focus on the fun they had, and not on their negative experiences. It's a time when older people can expose and break free from all the old skeletons in the closet. Michael and Billy were old men who could enjoy each other again in the carefree life pattens of two 20-year-olds. For a few days they were young again. For a few days their religious identities didn't matter at all.

Second, it occurred to me that life is like a stage play where the early acts lay a foundation for the ultimate meaning of our *entire performance on earth*. In Belfast, there had been many events that had separated people during those formative years. But remembering a cross-community friendship of long ago could knock down some of those sectarian barriers. At 84 years of age, Michael and Billy were no doubt aware that this might be close to the final scene of their real life-production. It seemed to give each of them a final chance to rethink their lives in a backdrop of joy and friendship.

They both died in the same year. In their own way, they each had a second chance to rise above their sectarian past.

19. A Lost Irish Love

This is another tale about my friend Michael the Trappist monk, and a love relationship that was cut short. As you may remember, Michael was born and raised in the South of Ireland. He grew up on a small farm in a part of the country that was made up entirely of Catholic families. In his early years, Michael's life was spent in a highly-structured environment. The Catholic Church was dominant in every aspect of his Irish society.

There were local dances for the young people, but even there the Church was very much in control. Michael said a priest attended all the dances to watch so that young people didn't get too close physically while they were dancing. But the local boys caught on how to fool the priest. They danced with their girlfriends like someone would dance with their mother. The priest soon got bored and went home. Then, the boys and girls could then dance close and enjoy themselves.

There was one dance, however, that Michael remembered above all others. It was the evening that he met Claire for the first time. He said he looked across the dancefloor and saw a young woman that had "a light" surrounding her. Michael was drawn to her like no other person he had ever met. He was a shy farm boy, but he pulled himself together and asked her to dance. Fortunately, the priest was gone by now so they could touch each other in a personal way. The dance transformed his feelings. He said he knew immediately that he loved this young woman and that he wanted to spend his life with her.

At the next dance a few weeks later, the two of them had the opportunity to go outside the dance hall and talk. Claire said she felt the same way about Michael. She knew he was the man for her. From that time on, the two of them met whenever they could. When telling me about this time in his life, Michael got a dreamy far-off look in his face. During that time, he thought about Claire every day. Their friends were nearly certain that Michael and Claire would marry one day.

But all of this took place in the early 1940s. The Republic of Ireland was a neutral nation so they were not involved in World War II. Northern Ireland, however, was British and therefore it was important in building British warships and aircraft engines. The German air force bombed Belfast on a regular basis causing much destruction. There was a shortage of young men in the North that could repair the bomb damage, so there was an opportunity for farm boys like Michael to travel to Belfast and earn much more than they could back home.

Michael spent nearly three years in Belfast. At first, he went back home to see Claire every weekend, but their times apart grew longer. Each time they were together they still had that special feeling of being in love, but they were spending a lot of time separated from each other. They both planned to be together after the war when Michael came home for good.

But Michael started to question whether he really wanted to live in Europe after the War. He told me that he believed there would be a third world war someday that would engulf Europe again and he really wanted to go to the United States. Claire, however, had no interest in leaving Ireland. Her family was a much more important part of her life. The two of them were never able to resolve the issue. Michael said they argued repeatedly about leaving Ireland. Claire finally said she would be willing to move to England. For a time, the compromise seemed to be acceptable to Michael.

But after the War ended, Michael moved to England where he finally ended up in an unskilled labor job in Birmingham. He said he never liked being around the British and he didn't really like the job. His mind was still on the United States, but his lack of skills made it difficult to emigrate to America. At that time, it was comparatively easy to enter Canada. It wasn't long before he decided to complete the Canadian immigration forms. Michael said the decision to leave Ireland was the most difficult of his life. Without Claire's knowledge, he booked passage on a ship that would sail from England to Canada.

Michael went back from England to Ireland one last time to see Claire. It was not a pleasant meeting. She pleaded with him, asking again if he would stay in Ireland or England. Michael said it was the most difficult day in his life when he told Claire that he was leaving for Canada. He said he hoped she would change her mind and come to Canada, but she didn't want to leave her family. It was a tearful good-bye as he boarded the ferry to go back to England in preparation for his trip to Canada.

It was a clear, crisp day when Michael arrived at the bus station in Toronto. But it wasn't long before he felt unwelcomed. When he filled out an application for employment in Canada, the comment was, "So your name is Farrelly. That's Irish. You're not qualified for this job." Michael said there was a sizable Irish community in Toronto, but he was reminded also of the discrimination in Northern Ireland. Some of the Protestants in Canada were very anti-Irish as well. The only jobs open to him were unskilled jobs in the construction trade. For a time, he was sorry that he left Ireland, but he was determined to make a life for himself in Canada, or maybe in the United States.

Michael said it was easy to cross the Canadian border into the United States. Nobody asked him any questions and he didn't feel the need to document his move. It was the late 1940s and jobs were plentiful. He finally ended up in Chicago, where he got a job bartending in a downtown hotel. Apparently, he learned how to mix all the drinks quickly because he received many generous tips from the regular customers. Michael loved every minute of the interplay between himself and customers in the downtown hotel barroom. It sounded to me that Michael was the typical jovial Irish bartender who got along well with everyone.

But Michael's interests also shifted to American sports. During his first summer in Chicago, he fell in love with baseball. At first, he didn't understand the rules of the game, but later he asked questions and finally he started going to the local ballpark as often as he could. It wasn't long before Michael became a Chicago Cub fan. He said the highlight of his experience was seeing Joe DiMaggio and Ted Williams play when they came to Chicago in an exhibition game. Michael said he became a "true American" when he went to the baseball park. He had a sparkle in his eye as he talked about baseball, his new love in America.

But Michael still thought a lot about Claire during these times, but he didn't think he would ever go back to Ireland. He had a regular correspondence with his sister and learned that Claire had married a local man. She and her husband lived just a short distance from where she and Michael had first met. He found out through his sister that Claire had two sons and seemed to be happy with her life. He was still thinking about his love for the girl he left behind. Michael said he tried not to think about her because he knew there was nothing he could do.

It was during this time, that Michael first read Thomas Merton's book,

Seven Storey Mountain. It was a celebrated autobiography of a man who gave up his life as a party-going intellectual in New York City to devote himself to God as a Trappist Monk. The book was credited with increasing a number of vocations inside the Catholic Church. It was extremely popular in post-World War II America where a new generation was looking for a satisfying spiritual direction. The Trappist order of the time was known for a contemplative life style and maintaining prolonged silence in their monastery. Thomas Merton gained a world-wide following among people who were inspired to read how a man could find his spiritual fulfillment in a life of silence, solitude, and poverty.

Michael had been an active Catholic all his life and he told me the Merton book had a personal meaning for him. In the back of his mind, he had always thought about living a monastic life. After reading Merton's book, he contacted several monasteries and found that they preferred prospective members to be younger than he was at the time. Finally, there was a positive response from Our Lady of Guadalupe Trappist Abbey in Lafayette, Oregon. Michael went to Oregon in 1955 and was accepted into the Monastery. He told me that he soon grew accustomed to life in the cloistered abbey where there was complete silence for hours at a time. He said it empowered him spiritually to spend hours in a contemplative state.

By the time I met Michael in 1991 the rules of silence at the Abbey had been relaxed somewhat, but the monks still spoke only when it was necessary. Despite the Trappist rules of silence, he and I met privately every Sunday afternoon in a small room at the Abbey where we could talk about any topic we pleased. Once a week we got together when I was in Oregon over a period of 19 years. He told me things about his life that he had never shared with anyone else. The two of us talked about everything. We had good times together.

Several times he discussed the love he felt for Claire as he wondered how she was doing back home in Ireland. All of that was to change, however, when Claire broke a 30-year silence and wrote him a very personal letter.

In a rather long letter, she told Michael she was now a widow and her two sons were married and were living on their own. She said she had loved Michael for more than 40 years and now she had a plan to bring them back together. Claire proposed that Michael leave the Trappist Abbey and move back to Ireland to be with her. She said she had a nice home and enough money for the two of them to live comfortably for the rest of their lives. Claire suggested that they should discuss it by mail and make a decision together that would be the best for both of them.

Michael read and reread the letter from Claire. It was only after two weeks that he shared the letter with me. I read the entire message from Claire while Michael sat there with tears in his eyes. She had written the letter carefully, arguing that their love for each other had been inspired by God, so they could come back together while remaining faithful Catholics.

It was clear that she anticipated Michael's religious reservations, but she concluded that they would be married in the Church and live out their days as God had intended. She was even willing to send enough money so Michael could buy a one-way commercial airline ticket to Dublin where she would pick him up, and together they would go to their new home in County Meath.

Claire sent a recent picture of herself which he looked at again and again. Her proposal put him in a crisis state. On the one hand, his love for her was as strong as ever. There was a flood of memories from their times together. He said he could see her face every time he closed his eyes. On the other hand, Michael had taken an oath of obedience and poverty as a Trappist monk. He said there was no way he could set his vocation aside and still be faithful to God. I don't think he ever seriously considered leaving the Trappist Abbey, but he couldn't bring himself to tell her "No."

From what I could see, his real task was how to handle the matter without appearing to be heartless. If possible, he wanted to let her down gently. But he was still in love with her. He could think of nothing else. The situation must have been on his mind day and night.

Michael said he went back and reread parts of *Seven Storey Mountain* where Thomas Merton had faced a similar problem of falling in love with a woman while he was a Trappist Monk. Merton actually had an affair and wrote at length about how he thought of his lover every day. He had a real problem getting his mind back to staying obedient to his oath as a monk. Michael read me portions of the book and I was struck by the similarity of the two situations.

The internal conflict went on for several weeks. Then he wrote one brief letter to Claire, saying that he couldn't see a way to proceed that would enable him to stay in the Church after he broke his sacred vow he took when he became a monk. He promised to write again after thinking more about the situation.

He finally came up with a solution that he shared with me before he acted. He decided to write a letter back to Claire, saying that he would love her forever, but that he had a very vivid dream in which he was told that his vocation as a monk was forever, and that it could not be broken. He also said the Abbot of the Monastery had noticed the letter from Claire and reminded Michael that he shouldn't write letters to anyone outside his own family.

In truth, there was no vivid dream about his vocation, also the Abbot had not commented on the letter, but Michael saw it as a way to take the matter out of his hands. As time went on, I inquired if Claire had sent any more letters. The answer was always "No." But each time I asked, I noticed Michael seemed more annoyed at my curiosity. The whole subject became very sensitive for him. He wanted to close the matter and not discuss it anymore with me, but his love for Claire never seemed to go away. It was clear to me that Claire was always on his mind. He was no longer the carefree man I once knew.

Several months after his contact with Claire, Michael went through a personal crisis that changed his outlook on life. Early one morning he slipped and fell on his way to Mass and could not get up. He was not found for nearly an hour. The medical examination did not show any serious injury, but Michael underwent a transformation that utterly surprised me. The next time I visited him, he told me he didn't want to see me anymore on Sunday afternoons. According to him, we were talking about things that were a "distraction" for him. Michael said he wanted to focus on his eternal soul, and did not want to spend time talking to me about sports and politics. He didn't want to discuss his life in Ireland anymore.

Driving home that afternoon from the Abbey, I thought maybe this was a temporary situation that would be remedied by rest. But the next time I tried to visit him he made a dramatic movement sweeping his arms together as he shouted, "We're through, Bill. Don't ever come back again."

I was heartbroken. I had lost my best friend in a way I could not understand. I didn't know what to do. I played the scene over and over in my mind.

What was wrong with Michael? I never saw him act this way before. What could I do?

I decided that there was nothing I could do. It was all up to him. All I could do was to wait. Maybe he would change his mind and we could be together again.

Two weeks went by before one of the other monks I knew contacted me by telephone to say, "We heard how he treated you and said we are sorry." The other monks had nothing to add except that Michael had become a "different person." Many of them had noticed the unexplainable changes in his personality. They said he didn't smile anymore, that he kept to himself in his own room at the Abbey.

I did not go back to the Abbey again. Michael died shortly after I saw him the last time. All I knew was that he had apparently died in his sleep. I was not told immediately of his passing, so I wasn't able to attend his funeral. I always wondered if the contact with Claire had anything to do with his change in behavior. I never did understand why he turned on me with such anger. Before the letter, Michael always had a smile on his face. He charmed everyone who met him. Why the change? Was he angry with me because I kept asking if he'd heard from Claire?

Before Michael's fall we had talked extensively about his feelings. He said the letter from Claire had changed everything. Now she was on his mind all the time. I could hear a sound of desperation in his voice. His eyes were often red from crying.

The thought occurred to me later that possibly Michael died of a broken heart. Maybe he couldn't stand to live any longer. I'll never know.

20. What's it All About?*

Much of my time in Belfast was spent in the small sectarian neighborhoods where unsightly 25-foot walls divided folks of the opposing religious communities. There were more than 80 specific localities in the city that were identified as being either totally Catholic or completely Protestant. Some were small embattled areas that have been invaded by the opposing side, so folks were careful to guard against a dangerous situation that might arise at any time of the day or night. There were armed people in each neighborhood. Everyone had a watchful eye.

I soon got to know the routine of these sectarian neighborhoods. Protestant and Catholic children went off to separate schools each morning. They all wore school uniforms so it was easy to tell them apart. More than 90 percent of these students went to schools that were identified with their own nationality. The Irish Tricolor flag was on display inside the Catholic schools and the British Union Jack was out front of the Protestant schools.

All the young people lived in their own sectarian world where they could hear and repeat an endless number of stories that dehumanized the kids on the other side. It sounded to me like the type of conversations that would take place in a locker room when teenage children traded half-stories they have heard from older kids. Most of these students never had a chance to interact with children from the other community. They lived an isolated life where everyone stayed in their place.

After school, these Belfast youngsters often engaged in the low-level sectarian activities by throwing rocks and bottles over the neighborhood walls. Even though they never met the kids on the other side, they all had sectarian nick-names for each other. Much of life seemed like a staged rehearsal to reinforce membership in their own tribe. Stories were told on each side that focused on how "different" they were from "us." Each side had their own cultural traditions complete with their own mythology, history, music, football teams, pubs, social clubs, political parties, and paramilitary armies. The street curbs were painted red, white, and blue in the Protestant part of town. In Catholic neighborhoods they were green, white, and gold. Everyone grew up in a highly structured environment with little or no appreciation for what life was like on the other side.

I was invited into many of the schools and spoke to the students about the United States. While the young people were friendly with me, it was clear that their schools had isolated them from the folks across town. The elementary and secondary schools in the North were an important part of the socialization process. In the absence of personal experience with the other side, there were a lot of doubtful stories that were repeated again and again. A young person born into this kind of religious tradition and was expected to stay there for all their time on earth. They could have a full life of 70 or 80 years and never have friends from the "other part of town."

Some of the British officials came up with plans to break down the sectarian division between young people. One of the earliest efforts was to sponsor a football (soccer) game so the boys might get to know each other on the playing field. There was a hope that the competition on the field might ripen into cross-community friendships. This was tried only once because both sides saw it as a chance to attack each other on the field. I met one young man who was involved in the one and only first game. He said, "We nearly kicked each other to death before they pulled us apart."

Then the government sponsored combined school class trips to visit a museum or planetarium under the supervision of teachers from both sides. This didn't work well either because the children and their teachers didn't even want to be in the same room. The opposing mythology was so strong that they were reluctant to stand together or talk to each other. Each peer group set down a fairly clear border between the two groups. No one dared to cross over and make friends.

Finally, an organization was formed that took the children out of Northern Ireland in cross-community pairs and sent them to the Netherlands where they spent a few weeks with a host family. I was on the board of the *Northern Ireland Holiday Scheme*, and the initial reports we had were favorable. We found that Catholic and Protestant teenagers could get along reasonably well as roommates away from home as long as the peer group weren't involved. But a problem arose when they came back to Northern Ireland and found they could not continue their relationship because they were afraid that they would be beaten up if they crossed the sectarian boundary line into an opposing neighborhood.

I became involved in an alternative plan. We arranged to take a small mixed group to the United States to see if they could forge friendships that might last when they returned to Belfast. A lot of planning went into the project. The British government funded the program.

I brought over a group of 14 teenagers (7 from each tradition). There was an equal number of boys and girls that were 15 and 16 years old. They flew from Belfast to Portland, where I took them to their dormitory rooms at the University of Portland. Father Wheeler, a Catholic priest at the University, agreed to supervise their overnight times on the campus while I was in charge of their daytime activities. Surprisingly, the Protestants thought the priest was a great guy because he bought them a pizza on their first night in Portland. Some of the Protestants said it was hard to call him "Father," but other than that, everything worked very well.

We spent a good deal of time around Portland. I tried to take them to see things that would be outside their experiences in Belfast. But perhaps their most *educational day* was a visit to the Mexican-American Cultural Center in Cornelius, Oregon, which was about 50 percent Hispanic, and was located about 25 miles west of Portland. It was planned as a chance to become aware of the diversity in Oregon, but surprisingly the visit turned out to be a *test* on whether the kids from Northern Ireland really understood the causes of their *own* conflict back home.

There were about an equal number of Hispanic and Ulster teenagers in a large room. I introduced the session with the invitation to open the floor for questions from both sides. At first the questions were general in nature, like "What is your neighborhood like?" or "What is the weather like there?" But then an especially articulate young Hispanic youth asked, "What is that conflict in Northern Ireland all about?" He followed it up with another searching question, "Why is there so much fighting in Belfast?" Now all of a sudden, the conversation got serious.

To the surprise of everyone, the combined group of Protestants and Catholics couldn't come up with a good answer. At first, they said, "We just can't get along with each other," and then the point was made, "We really hate folks on the other side." Then there was a moment when the young Mexican seized the moment and said, "But why are you killing each other?" There was more stuttering and repeating the same general comments about how the two sides have been fighting for hundreds of years. To the surprise of every-one, the young Mexican-American kid became even more assertive saying, "You really don't know, do you?" There was a silence in the room. The young Catholics and Protestants from Belfast were very uncomfortable. They didn't have an answer.

In our 15-passenger van going home that afternoon near Portland, my northern Irish teenagers were unusually quiet. None of them turned on the radio to hear the rock music. They just sat there looking out the window. When we stopped, I asked them to talk about their session with the Mex-ican-Americans and their inability to explain the conflict. They said they "didn't know where to start," that there were "so many things," they couldn't put their finger on the "real reason." Then the topic turned to what they should have given as the reason. But they still couldn't come up with a good answer. It was beginning to upset them. They said no one ever asked them that question before.

It occurred to me that back in Belfast, no one ever did ask that basic question. There were so many terrible stories on both sides that no one ever tried to be more specific about the *real reason* why the conflict has gone on for hundreds of years. Many folks will go on to tell you the conflict pro-vides everyone with a political/religious identity, it decides where you can live, where you go to school, who you marry, where you can get a job, it de-cides which paramilitary army you might join, and finally it decides where you are buried after you die, but no one could come up with a comprehen-sive answer that explained what the conflict was all about or why it seemed to have no end in sight.

One of my colleagues at The Queen's University of Belfast, Frank Wright, told me one day: "The conflict in Northern Ireland is about every-thing and nothing." The "everything" relates to all the divisive mythological factors that cover nearly all the subjects they could think of. The "nothing" refers to the fact that the major issues are so ill-defined that they are nearly impossible to articulate. The important point was that the working-class peo-ple of Belfast can't tell you in one phrase why they are so obsessed with the conflict, but it remains as the most important issue of their lives.

For me, the high point of that whole trip with Irish teenagers from Belfast to Portland was the visit to the Mexican-American Cultural Center.

I played the verbal exchange through my head many times as I remembered the uncomfortable response from the Belfast teenagers from both communities. I could see that they all felt frustrated because they couldn't answer the question. When I got back to Northern Ireland, I shared the story with both Catholic and Protestant adults. They just shook their heads, but they didn't offer an answer either.

In more recent times, I've been wondering how a group of American adults would respond if they were questioned about the political/cultural conflict in the United States. How would they respond to the question, "What's it all about?" Would they talk about which side won the election of 2020? What would they say about disagreements that have split American families? Would the attempted coup d'état of January 6, 2021 come up? What would be the explanation of why American society has become so polarized?

It may be interesting for folks in the United States to hear that the northern Irish can't understand either why American society is being pulled apart as never before. They were completely surprised by hearing about the kinds of issues that divides the US from the White House down to local school boards.

My friends in Ulster were amazed to see that a growing number of Americans no longer seemed willing to defend democratic institutions. In the past, many folks in Northern Ireland saw America as a stable democracy that was respected around the world. Belfast people (on both sides) are now alarmed at what has happened in the United States.

The last time I was in Northern Ireland I noticed an improvement in community relationships. The walls were still there, but there was a growing openness among the embattled neighborhoods. When I came back to US, I noticed things were getting worse. The United States was becoming more like the old Belfast where there was a tension in the air that no one could explain.

The conflict in the United States is becoming more about "everything and nothing." It's about all sorts of things that turns folks against each other, but underneath it's about "nothing you can put your finger on." Maybe it's time to take small groups of Americans to Belfast where they could get away from the irrational things that divide them.

I wonder what that American group would say if a northern Irish kid would ask them, "What's it all about?"*

A version of this chapter appeared in a book I wrote earlier. Bill Meulemans, *Dynamiting the Siskiyou Pass and Other Short Stories from Oregon and Beyond* (Ashland, Oregon: Hellgate Press. 2023) pp. 189-196.

21. They're All Going to Hell

Several years ago, I attended an Irish Association meeting in what was then Northern Ireland's second largest city. Protestants referred to it as "Londonderry," but Catholics always called it "Derry." The city was considered to be just a little bit safer than Belfast for a mixed meeting of Catholics and Protestants.

The Irish Association was made up of mostly university-educated, middle-class, political, economic, and cultural leaders from both the North and South of Ireland. One of the main purposes of the Association was to try to bridge the gap between the competing sectarian communities of the North. The organization had a neutral reputation across the entire island. I expected the meeting would be low-keyed event where everyone was soft spoken and non-sectarian in their approach to life. I certainly didn't expect any major disagreements.

Two of the speakers on the program that day were John Hume, leader of the Social Democratic and Labour Party (SDLP) and Gregory Campbell of the Democratic Unionist Party (DUP). Both men were from Londonderry (Derry) and were well-known throughout the province. Hume was the leading moderate on the Catholic side that favored power-sharing between the two communities. Campbell was known for his strong insistence to minimize the Catholic role in the North. He was an outspoken Protestant who was a prominent member of the Free Presbyterian Church founded by the Reverend Ian Paisley.

Hume spoke first. I could tell he was unprepared as he wandered around the subject of the conflict. He finally reflected on the element of chance when he said that he happened to be born a Catholic while Gregory had been born a Protestant. Hume went on to say, "Isn't it a shame that Gregory and I are on opposing sides in this battle because of an "accident of birth." Hume concluded by saying that if people thought about this throughout the North of Ireland maybe they could knock down some of the barriers of sectarianism that divided them and learn to live together. John Hume sat down thinking he had at least made a positive statement.

Campbell got to his feet quickly as though he had something important to say. He began by saying that Hume's remarks were the most "disgusting ideas" he had ever heard. He went on to say that people are not born Protestant "out of chance," that God does not offer salvation by "accident of birth." Campbell went on to say that the differences between the two peoples in Ireland were the divisions between "good and evil," and "light and darkness." The implication was that God intended that some people were going to Heaven and others were bound to go to Hell. He concluded by banging his fist on the podium and declaring, "You can't trivialize religion by saying it's just an accident of birth!"

I was surprised by the sweeping nature of Campbell's assertions, and I remember thinking to myself that his comments were entirely out-of-bounds, and that those ideas would not be accepted by any other of the Irish Association members. I couldn't imagine that anyone in this "neutral body" would agree with condemning all the members of the Catholic Church to Hell.

But to my surprise, the Protestants in the room stood up an applauded. They strongly agreed with Campbell as they focused on how God had ordained certain people to be born Protestants and that salvation was predetermined, not just something decided by chance. In response, the Catholics in the room rose from their seats in strong disagreement and loudly denied that salvation was exclusive to one religion. Everyone was talking at once – no one was listening to anyone else.

It was almost like watching time lurching back five-hundred years when the two religions were caught up in an endless bloody battle. I felt like I was hearing voices from the Reformation as some claimed an exclusive relationship with God. I was one of the few people in the room still sitting down. Everyone else was standing up, waving their arms, raising their voices and moving around in a semi-aggressive manner. No punches were thrown, but a couple of men did push each other. I looked over at the journalist who was sitting there shaking his head.

The loud exchange of sectarianism nearly broke up the conference. Someone suggested it was time to break for lunch. People dispersed into two separate huddles as they continued to support their own religious tradition. In a real sense, they were still coping with the issue that has divided them for hundreds of years: who was going to be saved, and who was going to go to Hell?

The sectarian melee ended as quickly as it started. After 10 or 15 minutes, there was suddenly a loud silence in the room as everyone came to their senses. They all started looking at the floor as if they were ashamed to look at each other. Their anti-sectarian, middle-class values must have kicked in. They knew they shouldn't have acted that way.

There were no name tags on the lunch tables, but I noticed a rather "churchy" atmosphere with all the Catholics seated at their own tables while the Protestants were all together at their own place. There was no chatter. Everyone just sat there and ate their salads.

The program after lunch was rather low-keyed with a weak discussion about reducing the tensions at the schools that were segregated by religion. Even the well-known political leaders from the North and South had nothing of real interest to say. In watching the meeting, I was reminded of how a group of children would act after a shouting match. They would all know they had misbehaved in public and they each would feel a little embarrassed.

The meeting ended early. Everyone left the room quietly and went home.

Before that day, I considered the Irish Association to be the best hope of the future. They were the "movers and shakers" of Ireland, the ones who were the voices of reason in a country that needed to be healed after decades of division. They were supposed to be "the adults in the room." There were newspaper publishers, heads of large companies, television personalities, university presidents, and leaders of all descriptions. Their names were well-known to everyone north and south of the border.

I guess I felt the Irish Association was above all this. They were *not* linked to the paramilitaries of either side. They were all so moderate in public, and they were the ones that supported cross-community activities. I think most people felt these recognized leaders were not tainted by the sectarian attitudes of the working-class who were out on the streets doing the fighting and the dying.

But it looked to me that day, deep down, the community leaders in the Irish Association had the same sectarian prejudices as the folks in the working-class ghettos; they just were able to cover it up better. These leaders were dressed in a more respectable manner, had larger vocabularies, spoke with more conventional grammar, but underneath they were much the same as their counter-parts who were involved in violence. This was a surprise to me.

I thought they was a collection of "neutral" people who could serve as an example to the greater number of northern Irish on both sides.

That evening as I drove back to Belfast, I thought long and hard about how the conflict was like an iceberg – only a part of it was visible above the waterline. Most of it was covered up inside of people's minds. I think the Irish Association members would agree with that assessment because *they looked so utterly surprised after they attacked each other.* They didn't seem to know that they could collectively be swept back that quickly into the Reformation. It all happened in a flash.

Then I started thinking about the ordinary Irish people on both sides, and how they treated me with so much generosity and kindness. With all those positive characteristics, how could they harbor so much sectarian anger for each other. I will never forget the look of complete disgust on Gregory Campbell's face as he defended his version of a spiritual salvation for Protestants. Also, I won't forget hearing John Hume (sitting next to me) mutter under his breath, "You f—-ing bigot!" as he listened to Campbell. Perhaps the two of them had stumbled on the issue that was always lurking down deep in Ulster history. Maybe it was deeper and more pervasive than I ever imagined.

It passes easily to say that neither side has taken the time to understand the other, but that would not be true. It is also said too often that neither side listens to the other, but that's not true either. How can reasonably intelligent, well-informed people live so close together and still feel that way about each other? Why?

As I was driving back to Belfast that evening, I started thinking about the United States – about how we were caught in a similar situation where there was so much below the waterline that divided us. Did I think the "movers and shakers" in towns across America were similar to their counterparts in the Irish Association? Did I suspect there were terrible, divisive attitudes lurking just below the surface even with the local leaders who supposedly were "above" the conflict?

But then I thought the US doesn't have a history of sectarianism, so why are we so divided? How could it happen here? We Americans, think we are far above tribal thinking. Are we really? There was a time not long ago when we declared that we lived in the "United States," and we emphasized the word "United." In some people's minds that's no longer true. Red and Blue are not just a handy way to describe different points of view – those colors have come to define us.

Right now, the northern Irish are making some progress toward power-sharing. Some never thought they could put their guns and bombs aside and work through a democratic government. The future of Belfast now seems a wee bit more positive than it was 20 years ago. There have been some missteps along the way, but there is a guarded optimism in Northern Ireland. I wish I could say the same thing about the United States.

22. A Dangerous Coincidence

After I'd been in the North of Ireland for a while, I found I could pick up different accents in a crowded room between folks from different Belfast neighborhoods and others who came in from the outside. One particular day, my ears perked up because I heard the unmistakable voice of a guy from Boston who was working on a job in downtown Belfast.

I introduced myself to the man from Boston and found that he lived with his wife in a small town north of Belfast. I'll use the fictitious name of *Ben Green* for my new friend because I want to protect him from those – who I was to find out later – were trying to kill him.

Ben Green and I hit it off immediately. At our first meeting he told me the incredible story of his life and how he ended up in Ulster. Several years before, Ben had been awarded a scholarship to study in France. He had been in France for nearly a year when, by chance, he met a northern Irish woman I'll call Rose who was visiting France on a holiday. Ben said it was a remarkable occasion when they looked at each other for the first time because there was an immediate feeling between them that they were meant to be together. In his words, it was "love at first sight."

It must have been a wonderful courtship between Ben and Rose. While in France, they decided within a few days that they wanted to marry and find a new home. Rose didn't want to go back to Northern Ireland, but she had no interest living in Boston. She finally decided that she would consent to live in a part of the United States where there were a lot of green hills that were similar to northeastern Ireland. Ben had traveled around the American west and he advised her that Eugene, Oregon was very much like the green hills of County Antrim in Ireland. Within a few weeks, they traveled to the United States to begin their life in Oregon.

Rose had one other condition. She told Ben that they would live in Oregon for six months to try it out, and if she was not happy, he would agree to settle in Northern Ireland. Apparently, Eugene, Oregon did not meet her expectations because the two of them left Oregon after a few months and moved to a small town north of Belfast. Ben was then hired to a position where his American background was an asset.

During the next few months, I met Rose and I visited the two of them at their home. They delighted in retelling me the story of how they met, how they fell in love, and how they both had found happiness. We also talked about their time in Oregon and their adventures among friends who worked in the timber industry. It turned out that I had spent time in many of the same places in Oregon. They had enjoyed some of the same restaurants in Portland and Eugene that I knew well. It all seemed like a wonderful coincidence that we shared the Oregon experience and our friendship in Northern Ireland.

All of that was to change one evening when I met a man in a Belfast pub who had a different view of Ben and Rose. When he heard my American accent, he approached me and said he wanted to ask me some questions. The man was very rude; he peppered me with a barrage of enquiries. His main interest was finding out if I knew or had met any other Americans in Belfast. He followed up his inquiry by asking if I knew of any American man who was with a northern Irish woman.

At first, I didn't feel the aggressive temperament of the man who was asking me all these questions, but soon I could tell this was not just an aimless asking about someone I might know. I immediately thought of Ben and Rose, but I sensed that there was some danger in this situation. The man pushed up against me in the booth where I was sitting and told me his name was Brian. I was put off by him. He violated my space and spoke in a very accusative way. Without asking if I was interested, he told me a long story that was obviously about my friends, Ben and Rose.

It turned out that Brian was the former brother-in-law of Rose, and he was driven to find her to "get even" for something she had done. His story was all about revenge. According to Brian, Rose had been married to Brian's brother in Northern Ireland, but after a domestic spat, Rose went off to France to "think" about their relationship. But she didn't come back to Ireland. According to the story, Rose had telephoned a woman friend of hers in Belfast and told her that she had met an American who swept her off her feet. Later Rose contacted her friend again and told her that the two of them had lived in Oregon for a time, but that she and her new-found American friend were coming back to live in Northern Ireland.

Brian said his family did not go to the police with this information or use any official channels to find Rose because her former husband decided to track her down and deal with the problem in "his own way." The situation became more serious when Rose's former husband failed to find Rose. He apparently went into a deep depression and finally killed himself with a handgun.

After this, the hunt to find Rose became an obsession. Brian said the suicide completely destroyed his family. Since the death of the deserted husband, his mother had "lost her senses" and had long periods where she cried without end. The father of the suicide victim had joined in with Brian as they spent months trying to find Rose to punish her. Brian told me their plan was to find Rose and her American partner and kill them both. He said they avoided any contact with the police so no one would ever suspect that they were involved in the planned assassination.

At that point, I could feel Brian becoming angrier and more aggressive. He said he had a duty to avenge his brother's death. His face was puffy red and his voice was loud. He used a lot of four-letter words. Other people in the pub looked over toward us in a disapproving manner. No one wanted to be near him or answer his questions. I think all of us sensed that Brian was a dangerous man on a violent mission.

I wondered why he had told me his story with all those details, but I didn't want to appear interested. I just shrugged my shoulders and turned away trying to appear that I cared nothing about the situation. But inside, I knew that Brian was crazed and would resort to violence if he had any idea I knew where Ben and Rose were living. He spoke to me in a manner that suggested that he suspected I knew something. I started to feel unsafe as Brian raged on and on.

My final response was something like, "I don't know anything about this situation. It's time for me to leave." I had to push Brian away because he was blocking my exit. When I left, Brian was still standing there, still in an excited state.

The next weekend I called Ben and Rose and asked if I could drop by to see them. It was time for me to warn them because — as it turned out — neither of them knew Brian was looking for them. Also, they did not know that Rose's former husband had killed himself. When I told them about my experience with Brian, there was an immediate look of fear in their eyes. I could tell right away that they were afraid for their lives.

They quickly apologized to me for not telling me that Rose was a married woman when the two of them met in France. In truth, Rose had abandoned her husband when she met Ben. She never bothered to get a divorce. Rose was really guilty of bigamy. In France she started going by a different name so that she could "leave her other life behind." She said her husband's family were very "intense people," and that she was afraid to face them. This was the reason why Rose and Ben were so careful to cover their tracks. But they had mistakenly believed that they could just "disappear" and never be found by Brian's family. They had intentionally picked a town several miles north of Belfast where they thought they were safe, but they were wrong.

We had a long talk and I reminded them that Brian had found me by chance, and that they were lucky that I wasn't the kind of person who would reveal their residence. I said if Brian kept looking for them, he would probably find them. He could just repeat his question over and over: "Do you know a man with an American accent who is living with a northern Irish woman?" It would just be a matter of time before someone would say: "Yeah, I know an American guy who lives with an Irish woman, and I know right where they live."

Then I told them that if they stayed in Ireland there was a high probability that they would be killed. I pointed out that Brian was an extremely violent man, and that there was little doubt in my mind that he would try to kill them both. I went on to say that Brian could pick his own time and place for the revenge killing. They would have little or no chance to resist him because he was driven to avenge his brother's death. After a few minutes, both Ben and Rose were convinced that they had to leave the country for their own safety.

The last time I saw Ben and Rose they had already made their plans to leave Ireland. They were *careful not to tell me where they were going*. I didn't want to know. They had thought it through and decided that Brian might find out that I had warned them and that he would come after me next. It was important that I did not know their final destination.

There were tears in their eyes as we embraced for the last time. They thanked me over and over for warning them and suggested that I might have saved their lives. As I look back, I'm inclined to agree with them. I'm convinced that some things happen for reasons that are beyond our comprehension.

At first, I was not able to understand why I was involved in this ill-fated situation. Why did I happen to meet Brian who was looking for them? Then I started to think that I may have had a destiny to warn Ben and Rose, and maybe this chance series of events saved their lives. It reaffirmed my belief that nothing happens by accident.

23. Why the Red Poppy Divides the North

I learned early that there's no sure way to tell a Protestant from a Catholic in downtown Belfast except during the first part of November. That's the time when nearly all patriotic Protestants wear a red poppy as a public way of remembering the veterans of the British military who gave their lives in combat. The tradition evolved out of World War I when a poet noted that colorful red poppies grew near the battlefields in Flanders that was strewn with the bodies of those who fought for a noble cause. Ask any Protestant and they will tell you that the red poppy today is a symbol of solemn remembrance of those who fought in all the wars of the past.

But I never met a Catholic in the six counties of Northern Ireland who would say the red poppy was just a "symbol of solemn remembrance." It was seen by some Irish nationalists I knew in the North as a symbol of British imperialism. They contended that wearing the poppy in November was a way the British can remind everyone of their dominance over the Irish people.

These two sides on this topic cannot be reconciled unless you go inside the heads of folks who have opposing views. It comes down to a feeling that comes automatically when each side sees the poppy. I offer these views only after asking scores of Irish Catholics and British Protestants what they think of when they see the red poppy. There was a marked difference between the two communities.

On the Protestant side, people often started out by saying they had a strong, but soft feeling of gratitude mixed with a sense of pride for those who fought to preserve their way of life. They say there is a quiet dignity in the brightness of the poppy that sums up what it means to be British. It is worn to demonstrate a remembrance for the people who made the ultimate sacrifice. There is a feeling of good will and silent patriotism that stirs feelings of national appreciation.

On the Catholic side, there is an immediate picture of what the British empire has done to the downtrodden peoples around the world. It highlights the struggle of the Irish people who have fought injustices for hundreds of years. For some, the poppy is just a reminder of the aggressive policies that criminalized a free people whose only crime was to fight for their independence from Britain. The red flower reminds some of the Irish that the people of Ireland will never rest until they are free of British rule.

The subject of the red poppy came up during the month of November every year as I attended the military banquet that was held at The Queen's University of Belfast. As far as I know, I was the only American person at the formal gathering that took place in the Great Hall each year to commemorate the armistice that ended the first world war. It appeared that everyone present was either a military veteran or someone with a strong sense of British patriotism. Unlike everyone else in the room, my credentials were that I had served in the US Army and I had a copy of my honorable discharge as proof of my brief, but rather uneventful military career.

Many of the attendees were in military uniform or they wore portions of their uniforms and ribbons and medals they earned in the service. They *all* wore the red poppy as a minimum example of their commitment. The fact that I did not wear a poppy was noticed by everyone around me. Soon after I entered the Great Hall, I was approached by a very dignified looking gentlemen I did not know and asked whether I was "British." When he heard I was an American, he gave me an odd look as though I certainly didn't fit in with his special group of patriots.

After attending the military banquet for the first time, I shared my experiences with some of my working-class friends from both sides. They were especially intrigued to hear that I was asked again and again why I did not wear a poppy. One of my Catholic friends came up with an unusual solution to the problem – he went into downtown Belfast and purchased a poppy. He then spray-painted the poppy with bright green paint. He said, "Now Bill you will fit in well with the other British unionists." I thanked him for his interest, but decided not to wear the green poppy to the banquet. I can only imagine what the response would have been from those folks who would not see the humor in wearing a green poppy.

I never knew why, but each year at the banquet I was seated next to the same people, who happened to be executives at the Ulster Bank of Belfast. They all knew each other and had been members of the Ulster Defence Regiment (UDR) which was a part-time volunteer military unit of Northern Ireland unionists. The UDR had the task of assisting the Royal Ulster Constabulary (RUC) which was the standard police force that was also staffed by

Protestants who favored British control of Northern Ireland. The UDR and the RUC saw themselves as defenders of British rule in the North. To the untrained eye, UDR members looked like regular British Army troops, but local folks on both sides knew the UDR were a local armed force that was devoted to maintaining Protestant rule in the North.

My contact with the UDR members at the military banquet was during some of the darkest days of the conflict, long before the cease-fire and the beginning of the power-sharing government. The UDR members at my table saw themselves as active members of what they called "the security forces." I found out later that some UDR members kept their guns at home when they were not on duty. This was an important fact because there were strict gun control laws that kept guns out of the hands of Irish nationalists who might be members of the IRA. The "legal guns" were all on one side of the conflict.

So here I was in the middle of the corporate elite of Belfast who were all volunteers in the UDR. Their first question each year was why I didn't wear a poppy? I told them I was "neutral," but that didn't satisfy them. They wondered how I could be neutral on "law and order" and "Irish terrorism?" They wanted to know if my parents were Irish? Did I have any connections to persons in the IRA or other "resistance organizations?" They never seemed to tire of asking me probing questions.

At times there four or five of the Ulster Bank executives who were peppering me with questions. I felt like the odd person who was strongly suspected of being on the "other side," but they just couldn't prove it. I really enjoyed the interchange and sparring around for answers to their questions. They wanted to know why I was in Belfast and what I knew about Irish Catholic nationalists. Did I know any of them personally? What were they really like? Were any of them in the IRA? Did I feel safe in "their" part of town?

The same questions came up repeatedly: Why wouldn't Catholics wear the poppy? Weren't they proud to be British, and why did they support the IRA? They all seemed very interested in the *real goals* of Irish nationalists. I was amazed by their lack of knowledge and their very slanted view of history. They were the educated corporate elite of Belfast, but they had completely swallowed the propaganda of the hard-core loyalist faction of Belfast Protestants. They kept asking me the same question over and over, "What do Irish nationalists really want?

My response was that the Irish nationalist's main goal was "equality." That they wanted to have the freedom to control their own country. There was an immediate strong negative response to me referring to "their own country." The all shouted at once, "Ulster is British." There was no agreement that they would ever share power with Catholics in the North.

Everyone at the table raised their voices as they dictated their terms for peace in Northern Ireland. These unionists at my table demanded that the IRA had to end the war first before there would be any talk of sharing power. I knew from my contacts with republicans that they wanted the political reforms to be put in place before they put the guns away. We had a lively negotiation at our table while people at the other tables were more silent and respectful; they might have noticed that all these questions were aimed at a guy who wasn't wearing a poppy.

The debate at our table finally came down to what Catholics in the North would have to do to promote a lasting peace. They would have to denounce all the Irish rebels that had fought the British for hundreds of years. (This of course would never fly with Irish republicans.) It occurred to me that the real goal of Ulster Protestants was to *humiliate any and all people who had ever fought for Irish independence.* I was astonished because these Ulster Protestants wanted to turn the clock back hundreds of years to a time when Irish Catholics were afraid personally to fight for the unification of North and South. The discussion gave me a lot to think about after the military banquet.

The focus at my table finally came down to the demand that I agree with them, that Northern Ireland was "British," that London would never permit Irish Catholics to become partners in the democratic process. These men from the Ulster Bank repeated the Protestant motto, "Not an inch." There could be no compromises in their intent to "Keep Ulster British." They kept pressing me to agree with them. But I just listened.

Later, I recounted this experience with Irish republicans I knew. I was not prepared for the anger that resulted as they heard what was said around the banquet table. Much of their concern was around the question of how British Protestants could claim to be promoting democracy around the world when they violated it so openly at home.

I heard the long account from Irish nationalists of how the British had colonized many people around the world, robbed them of their freedom and then demanded that they would respect the British government as the "mother of democracies." Then came the prediction that someday the Brits would "leave Ulster Protestants behind" as they did with other former colonies.

Members, and former members of the IRA (I met with after the military banquet) kept coming back to the point that all they really wanted was equality. Irish republicans had told me several times that they welcomed the Protestants staying in the North as long as people on both sides had equal standing before the law.

One evening after attending the annual military banquet and discussing the occasion with Irish nationalists, I started thinking about how both sides have depended on outsiders to explore and expose their inner values at a personal level. It is one of the great ironies of the Northern Ireland conflict that outsiders have often put their finger on the pulse of the people on each side in a manner that was widely appreciated by folks in that particular community.

Frank McGuinness, a Catholic from the South of Ireland wrote the play, *Observe the Sons of Ulster Marching Toward the Somme*. It was a highly emotional account of Ulster Protestant soldiers from Belfast in the British Army preparing for battle the night before going to their death on the 1916 battlefield at the Somme. Belfast Protestants have told me that this play, more than any other, speaks of their "pain" and willingness to die for "King and Country," and how important it was to never abandon the Protestant people in an Ireland dominated by "Catholics."

When I saw the play, I was surprised at the end (when the house lights came up) by how many people in the theater were weeping openly as they remembered how much Ulster had given to the British Empire, and how the present government in London was willing to let Irish Catholics have a greater role in governing the North. The Battle of the Somme in 1916 has always been remembered in Belfast as the time that illustrated the great Ulster Protestant sacrifice.

I recall an older Protestant woman telling me that after the Battle of the Somme, the telegraph boys brought a "dreadful message of death to nearly every house in Protestant West Belfast." The question has been asked by generations of Protestants: "How could their mother country abandon them now in a country with a majority of their eternal foes? More than 100 years have passed since World War I, but it still evokes an emotional memory.

On a comparable level, Leon Uris, an American Jew, wrote *Trinity,* a book which northern Catholics told me really captured the Irish psyche in respect to their nationalism and their deep anger toward British domination. When I visited the homes of Irish republicans, I often found *Trinity* to be on their bookshelves along with only a few other books. Several of them confided in me when they said that *Trinity* recounted their story in a way that brought tears to their eyes.

Former IRA prisoners told me that Bobby Sands (the first to die on hunger strike in 1981) had memorized long portions of *Trinity* and recited it out loud in the prison after the lights were out in the evening. I was told this particular long quotation was one of Bobby Sand's favorite passages:

> The enemy sits in mahogany rooms and makes up rules. By their rules they declare their legality to colonize people who don't want to be colonized, rules to conduct warfare by, rules to legally starve people to death, and rules to carry out whatever they want to carry out. They say with enormous pride, these rules come from the mother of Parliaments so obviously they must be right and anyone who goes against these rules must be wrong. We are expected, as a subject people to live by their rules, fight by their rules, and obey their rules. But we don't have an army or arms and cannot fight by their rules and as this struggle develops, we will have to make up our own rules. Now, according to their rules, we are depraved ... killers, fanatics, anarchists, gunmen, or whatever scum they so designate, and therefore fit to be destroyed by their self-declared legality. *

Reportedly, Bobby Sand's late-night recitations inspired other IRA prisoners to fight on. Many Irish republicans I know have read *Trinity* because it supplied them with a poetic justification for fighting the British. Few of them seemed to know the author was an American Jew.

Both sides see these literary works as telling their story as they would have told it, not realizing perhaps, that it came from someone outside of their own camp. Considering these two authors (neither of which was northern Irish) gives me reason to believe that an objective writer – who is not burdened down by personal involvement or nationality – can delve into a conflict in a manner that touches the collective soul of the people. It may surprise many to discover that an outsider has a real advantage when exploring a conflict that is so filled with raw human emotion.

---

*Leon Uris, *Trinity* (New York: Double Day, 1976). pp.129-30.

24. QUB Politics

Less than one-half of the members of the Politics Department at The Queen's University of Belfast were born and educated in Ireland. The majority were either English or Scottish. I was the only one born and educated in the United States, and some of them never let me forget it.

All 19 of us gathered for lunch together on Mondays at a long table. Frequently there would be a well-planned question from one end of the table aimed in my direction. "Tell me Bill, do you sometimes give your students in the States examinations during the semester?" My reply was, "Yes, sometimes two or three examinations during the semester." The statement from the other end of the table was, "Education must be terribly disjointed there. As you know, our students have sufficient time to integrate their education. We have an examination at the end of each academic year." The implication was that QUB students study all year long thereby gaining a well-integrated view of a subject while Ameican students just get unrelated bits and pieces every few weeks.

I decided to find out if my QUB students spend their time "integrating the whole year" so I asked them. I said to all of them (in a large lecture hall) with a smile on my face, "Just between the two of us, tell me how many of you wait to study until the last week or two before the examination?" About 80 percent of the hands went up. When I reported this at the next Monday luncheon, someone murmured, "Oh, that can't be true. They must have misunderstood what you were asking."

But at the same Monday lunch, came another cutting question, "Tell me Bill, isn't it difficult to do research in a country that is divided into such arbitrary periods of time for learning? We in the UK are recognized all over the world for research breakthroughs in so many academic disciplines." My response was "Then you must lead the world in Noble Prizes. Is that true?" At this point there was a bit of coughing and silence. I looked it up later and found that the United Kingdom had a little over 130 Nobel laureates in history while the United States had more than 400. I reported that fact at the next noon luncheon. There was an awkward silence.

Later, at a departmental meeting, one of the English-educated professors admonished me for encouraging questions during my lectures. One professor with a strong English accent said, "We were told that you actually ask students to react to something you say during a lecture. Is that true?" My answer was "Yes, I often ask for student reactions several times during each lecture." There was a look of disbelief around the room. I went on to say, "I want to know if the students understand the significance of what I am saying, and it tends to keep everyone alert as they get a chance to follow-up with additional questions."

I went on to say I did not know the 180 students in my lecture section by name, so I often called on them by saying, "You with the red sweater in the third row, what problems do you see with Americans spending that much money on presidential elections campaigns?" I usually got only a brief answer, but it kept everyone alert and encouraged them to think critically and ask questions in return.

But again, at the long departmental luncheon table, someone in the room wondered if it "was proper to allow questions during lectures." Another professor said he had been at the University for 14 years and had only been asked "two questions" during his lectures. He actually seemed to be proud that he did not arouse any curiosity in the classroom.

We also had a rather odd requirement at Queen's University in that the entire department would view each examination question from every faculty member. All 19 of us would sit around a large table and someone would read each of 30 or more questions out loud to see if anyone wanted a particular question rephrased with different words. I got the impression that we were encouraged to note any grammatical errors or factual mistakes in any of the questions.

In one of my questions, I used the term," Black voters." One of the female professors with a strong English accent said, "Bill, you mean to say "Negro voters, don't you?" I said "No, I mean to say Black voters." She went on say, "I do believe 'Negro' is the correct name." At this point, I raised my voice a little and said, "There have been many different publicly-used names during our history." Some of them, I indicated, I would not repeat because they are very racially provocative. I went on to say that the earliest name was "darkies," then it was "colored," next came "people of color," after that came "Negro," and finally the term "Black" is used the most often today." But the professor with the English accent would not give up. She said, "Several years ago I was in the States for three months, and I still think 'Negro' is the correct term." I countered by saying, "I've spent my entire life there and I know the word 'Black' is used most often, but thank you for your comment." A few of the professors who were born in Ireland snickered a bit. It seemed that this particular woman in the department thought she was an authority on nearly everything.

Perhaps the most interesting differences I had from the British model was the construction of essay questions. Their approach was to ask one question at the end of the year. For example, one of their typical questions in the Middle East course was: "The Israelis and Palestinians have many areas of disputes. Discuss." I thought this type of enquiry provided little direction for a student. Who would know for certain how to answer that question?

My approach was to ask my student to analyze, to search through many aspects of a situation and determine the probable importance of specific factors. For example, one of my questions was: "What are the major reasons why the US President cannot promote party discipline in the Congress? How does this situation discourage political accountability in government?"

Members of the department were nearly unanimous in asking me to shorten my questions. I stood my ground and insisted that I wanted students to apply their knowledge to specific situations and to evaluate the probable impact in the political process. They didn't quarrel with that statement, but they weren't happy with my longer questions.

I took another step that none of my colleagues knew about during my 11 years at QUB. I supplied my students with eight analytical study questions, with the added advice, that if they prepared to answer all these questions in detail, I expected they would "do well" in the examination at the end of the year.

I then instructed them how to draw information from their readings and lecture, and how to prepare each answer in a written form outside of class. My recommendation to them was to meet (in groups of three) to learn how other students in their small group were interpreting each question. This enabled them to "take apart" each question and search for all the underlying points of view. I taught them how to listen to each other, take notes, and how to debate the points that were being discussed within the group. The end result would be a well-reasoned answer to each of the eight questions. Then, I advised them to write out the entire eight answers with supporting examples for each major point. They wrote down everything I said. I'm pretty sure most of the them carried through with the process.

I told them that this method employed all their senses. They read about it, studied it, heard about it, debated it, thought about it, and finally wrote about it. I went on to say that because they had *tested* the information so thoroughly, that level of understanding would stay with them many years after they graduated. My concluding remarks were that was how I was taught to learn when I was in college, and why I know it works.

I told them this was to be an on-going process that would end with what might be a well-reasoned set of professionally-done articles that would explain a particular phase of American politics. My final comment to them was, "Because you have so much time to prepare thoroughly, I will be expecting a complete and thorough answer." In effect, I taught them how to write eight separate articles outside of class with supporting ideas and evidence.

My *unstated promise* to the students was that one of these questions would likely appear in the examination at the end of the year. To my knowledge, this teaching technique never "got out" to my fellow faculty members. My students apparently kept it a secret. The only report I received was that my students did better than any others in the department. My colleagues were visibly bothered by the high quality of my students' performance. Could it be that the "American upstarts" had some good ideas on how to teach?

I never shared this approach with the other professors at Queen's University because I know they would have forbidden me to use a method that was new to them. I don't think my system was inherently better, but I do think there should be room for different methods in the classroom. How else can we make progress unless we can try something different?

My course on American politics was an elective class not required for a degree, but it grew steadily in numbers during the 11 years while I was on the faculty. I began with about 80 students and it doubled after a few years. My students did not hesitate to let me know that they approved of the open approach and how I expected them to question me during the lecture. Before I got to know their names I would often say "You with the blue sweater, what do you think of the point I just raised? One student told me later "We all started wearing gray or other light-colored clothes to avoid being asked a question."

But there was a time when there were many questions. I had smaller groups of 15 students each in two tutorials on Monday and Tuesday morning. I got to know their names and some of the unique ideas they had about the United States. These were some of the most promising students I have ever encountered in my teaching career. They were very inquisitive. I always looked forward to sitting down at a conference table with these young men and women.

I was a bit surprised to learn that most of these people in small groups had a general sympathy for the United States. (This was long before the days of Donald Trump.) One day I was talking about the mistakes of US policies in Vietnam and Southeast Asia. After class two young men said to me, "Don't be so critical of your own country." Nearly every student I knew admired the open approach that Americans have in politics and life.

When the World Trade Center was hit on 9/11, my students and the other citizens I knew made a point out of personally offering me sympathy for those that were killed. It was at this time when the American Consulate in Belfast had the front of the building covered with flowers and notes of sympathy. I always said, "Ireland is one of the few places left in the world where the people *still like Americans.*"

I arrived back in Belfast just four days after 9/11. I accepted an interview on BBC Television in Belfast and was asked many sympathetic questions about how Americans were responding to the attack across the nation. In my judgment, it was the high point of accepting the United States as a special friend of the United Kingdom and Ireland. There was no sectarian division in the response from Ulster. The friendship was genuine and deeply felt by all, including Queen Elizabeth who went on television and sang along with others as they sang "God Bless America."

25. Different Ways of Thinking and Acting

The Linen Hall Library, founded in 1788, is the oldest library in Belfast. It is located in the city center just across the square from City Hall. The library prides itself in having the most extensive collection of materials dealing with the Northern Ireland conflict going back many years. Early on, librarians at the Linen Hall had the good sense to go out on the street to observe events and collect everything they found. Upstairs are stacks of pamphlets, newspapers, photos and recorded memories that are available to serious scholars from all over the world. The library has the most complete record of any major sectarian conflict of its kind.

The Linen Hall Library was my home away from home. Many a day I spent reading old newspapers and personal diaries, to learn that certain parts of the city have always been the scene of riots, bombings, and murders. I was looking for geographical patterns, and I soon found that the same street names and surnames popped up repeatedly. There was a certain predictive quality in the conflict as both sides returned again and again to the same behavior and practices on the same street corners. I discovered several parallel sectarian roots that were buried deep inside the city.

After a full day in the library, it seemed only natural to join other researchers as we gathered in a nearby pub to discuss recent political events. The Fountain Pub was located in an alley one block from the Linen Hall. There was a group of "regulars" who came in on specific days of the week. Late Tuesday afternoons were especially interesting – that's when there were three older men who sat in one corner discussing politics from an analytical point of view. One of them was an older retired Protestant secondary-school teacher from East Belfast who always wore a suit and tie. He had an extensive collection of materials at home that went back more than 100 years. The other two were former postal employees who grew up in the Catholic section of West Belfast; they both had sharp memories of how the current conflict had unfolded in their lifetimes.

Unlike folks out on the street, these three men were students of politics, not participants. Together, the four of us spent countless hours discussing the reasons why the current conflict had raged on for nearly four decades. We were always looking for new ways to understand what had occurred in the past, and what was happening in the present.

One day I made an off-handed comment to the group about how there was such a difference in how the two sides approached problem-solving. Without thinking about it too much, I said "the two sides actually seemed to think differently, they actually process information in a different manner." After I cited several examples, the other three men were inclined to agree with me.

That comment was the beginning of a research project that never ended for me. Over the next several years, these three men and myself dug deeper into the political/religious psychology of both communities. We talked to people we knew from both communities who continuously fell back into the familiar thinking patterns. Our intellectual goal was twofold: first to determine if the people in each community did indeed have a unique way of thinking that was common only to their group, and next to find out why? This is what we concluded:

When people are strongly influenced by sectarian institutions – as they are in Ulster – they learn not only to share the same religious beliefs, they also use the same method of reasoning that is prominent in their religious experiences. The result is that people begin to apply the same thought processes and methodologies learned in religion to their political world as well. This is especially true when religion and politics are so closely intertwined.

In Ulster, even people who don't go to church consider themselves to be "cultural members" of their religions, and they pick up the particular thinking patterns that are common within that tradition. It is this *cultural/psychological aspect* of reasoning that comes through in their politics. It's an easy and comfortable process to start thinking like other members of the tribe. Psychological habits of this kind usually begin in childhood.

In the Linen Hall Library, we listened to hours of taped interviews and found patterns that emerged repeatedly. It soon became apparent that *both religious communities approached their political problems from a very different perspective.* We determined that their differences may well be rooted in their religious histories. It was a tantalizing idea, that they were influenced by traditions that had been formed hundreds of years ago.

To begin with, we found that Ulster Protestants were very proud that they have *protested* against unacceptable religious practices of the past in the Medieval Christian Church. Breaking up and branching off from the main body was a time-honored tradition among Ulster Protestants. They were quick to voice their disagreements as they turned against their former leaders. They felt very comfortable starting a new church.

Irish Catholics, on the other hand, had built their faith around remaining loyal to their "Mother Church" – they were proud of *maintaining* a church that dated back two thousand years. There was no "protest" tradition we could see among Irish Catholics. They had, instead, a strong tendency to stay within an existing body, support their leaders, and keep their criticisms to themselves. The fact that others had "left" the Church, renewed their determination to "stay true" to the church of their birth. In some cases, Catholics may *leave* their Church, but they seldom start a new one.

It seemed evident that the differences in thought patterns between the two faiths dated back to the Reformation. In that period, Protestants expended a lot of energy defending their "religious legitimacy" as they split off from the larger body. They believed a relationship with God could be found by individuals outside the long-standing body of the prevailing Christian church. Catholics, however, defended "their legitimacy" by remaining inside the Church, and following the teachings of the established central body in their religious institution.

I was reminded of this difference nearly every time I spoke to political leaders of both communities. Protestants were always ready to break away and form a new group. Catholics, on the other hand, were more inclined to reform their organization from the inside. This difference was even noticeable among paramilitary groups. The Protestant UDA and UVF were always disagreeing and criticizing each other. Catholic members of the IRA usually kept most of their disagreements within their organizational family, or in a small group that shared their concern.

But I knew of a few cases when leading republicans would visit the homes of dissenters in the evenings and tell them to "stay in line or else..." But by comparison, members of the UDA and UVF often disagreed in public, sometimes they would threaten each other with weapons while everyone else looked on at a public press conference.

A similar pattern existed among political parties. Irish nationalists usually worked out things behind closed doors. Ulster unionists would often denounce each other in public. I was constantly amazed on how the two sides handled disagreements within their ranks. It was almost like both of them had a script that they followed from hundreds of years before. Each appeared to have historical roots that influenced their current behavior.

It was also clear that the Reformation left a contrasting sense of community between the two religious' traditions. I found that Protestants were much more individualistic in their approach to life while Catholics were more inclined to combine their efforts for the sake of the entire group. This showed up in all sorts of community organizations.

I remember that Catholics were the first to set up credit unions in their neighborhoods rather than going through established banks that usually refused them credit. Individual Catholics have told me that they never would have been able to buy a home if it had not been for the credit unions that "helped everyone." Protestants were slow to follow suit in this area. They are still inclined to approach most challenges of life without outside help. The belief in individual rights and being responsible for your own welfare is exceptionally strong among Protestants.

But perhaps the most noticeable philosophical difference was how Protestants and Catholics approached problem-solving. Catholic nationalists started out with broad generalized ideas and later moved toward particular issues. Protestant unionists, however, insisted that specific issues must be dealt with first before they would accept any broad conclusions.

The Reverend John Dunlop, a Protestant minister friend of mine said, "Protestants always read the small print of life." In fact, the first thing they do it to focus on the details, and they are very aware of all the specific things that could go wrong. But from my observations, Catholics read only the "chapter titles" that are in bold print; they usually begin a discussion with a broad idea they see as being correct, and then later consider less important issues that may be in doubt.

In short, the two today tend to approach political issues in much the same way as they do religious topics. Catholics, often begin a discussion of religion with what they regard as a known-truth: that they belong to the "one-true Church," and then they are ready to move later toward other details or issues. Protestants begin with a multitude of supporting biblical ideas and questions before they are willing to accept membership in what they would regard as an "authentic church." The two groups *begin their conversations at opposite ends and move in different directions.*

I have a close friend who is involved in organizing many cross-community projects. She says the difference came up every time they discussed a new problem. Catholic nationalists usually began with an assumption that a broad concept was agreeable and then dealt with specifics later. As expected, Protestant unionists moved in the opposite direction, starting with specific details first before they would consider any conclusions.

To a great extent, leaders from the two religious traditions have inherited their methods of political reasoning from their theological roots. Protestants often read their Bible every day. Catholics are less inclined to read the Bible.

Before the Reformation, the specific *general logic* of Augustine and Aquinas was prominent among early Christian philosophers. The most important feature of deductive thinking is that it moved *from a general set of principles to particular issues.* The process permitted a logical probing and defense of the original idea before discussion of minor issues. Catholics continued to employ this method when resolving disputes in other areas of life. They often began their thinking by starting out with a known fact or truth, and then move later to details or issues at a lesser level.

After the Reformation, however, Protestants were greatly influenced by the *inductive thinking patterns* of Luther and Calvin. The inductive approach *begins with sorting out specific facts first, and then moving toward a general conclusion later.* If the preliminary principles or issues were not acceptable, there would be no agreement in this process.

A prime example of these two approaches was apparent in the negotiations on the Good Friday Agreement (often called the Belfast Agreement). Catholic nationalists began with the broad assumption that Ireland was one country that should be united. Their approach was to search for a framework or process that would move them toward that general goal. Protestant unionists, in contrast, went immediately to the details about decommissioning of weapons, the release of prisoners, the assurance that the war was over, and a host of other thorny issues.

Throughout the negotiation, unionists were searching for an ironclad guarantee that the Union with Britain was secure. The often-repeated phrase of Protestants was "the devil was in the details." Catholics, on the other hand, were angling for a path that would lead them toward a "United Ireland." They were forever bringing up new ideas that would move them closer to their well-known goal. *The two sides suffered an impasse immediately.*

In current political affairs, Protestants often accuse Catholics of having ulterior motives or hidden agendas in their negotiations. They contend that Catholics might "bend the truth" to suit their needs at a particular time. Protestants see this practice as dishonorable and deceitful – Catholics just see it as a part of life. They contend that issues often merge together in their minds.

In addition, Irish Catholics often see things on a sliding-scale. There are a lot of gradations and gray areas in life that makes it difficult to pin down the relative importance of a particular issue. In the Catholic Church, even sin is divided between the *mortal,* and the less serious *venial.* Protestants are not convinced that evil deeds come in increments. Protestants have a low tolerance for uncertainty, they want to come to the main issue immediately.

In political affairs, Catholics are sometimes difficult to track, they often alter their stance because of changing circumstances. They may take a temporary position with a thought of moving in a different direction later. For Protestants, a commitment is forever, and they fear getting caught in what they call "the slippery slope" that might lead into a trap.

The contrasting temperaments of the two communities are also evident in how they open negotiations. Unionists are inclined to take an absolute and final position early in formal talks saying, "This has always been our position and it will never change." Republicans seldom make such a sweeping statement. This process of Protestants "showing their cards early" prompted a Catholic friend of mine to state that "he would love to play poker with them because they couldn't imagine anything that was not in their hand." He went on to say that unionists "tip their hand early in the game by starting out with their final bid."

On a related topic, just the thought of negotiations seemed to increase a sense of pessimism among Protestants. A favored tactic among them was to predict failure before they actually sat down at the table. It almost seemed like Protestant unionists were looking for ways to undermine the entire negotiation process before it began.

Typically, unionist negotiators led off with the most problematic issue first on the assumption that if the most difficult question couldn't be resolved, there was no need to consider any other points. Irish nationalists almost always want to take up minor issues first, with the hope that some momentum would build in the process that would make it possible to overcome the most difficult problem which would be considered last of all.

In negotiations, unionists saw the nationalist approach as manipulative and dishonest because it distracted attention away from the grave issues that unionists wanted to discuss first. Nationalists defended their approach as being optimistic and creative because they believed in leaving doors open to new possibilities that might evolve later. But Irish nationalist did this with a sly look on their face because they knew that their real objectives would be rejected immediately if these ideas were stated directly; they often have a twinkle in the eye as they "talk around" a topic without taking a specific stand.

Underlying all of this, nationalists seemed to have an almost natural inclination to mesh humor with serious political negotiations. In response to a question about the IRA, political leader Gerry Adams made his often-quoted statement, "They haven't gone away you know." To this day, Irish republicans repeat the phrase and laugh with glee, reflecting their delight at the not-so-secret meaning. The incident still makes unionists angry because they know the joke was on them.

26. Mark of the Beast

The Reverend Ian Paisley (1926-2014) probably did more to divide the two communities of Northern Ireland than any other person. He preached at length about the Catholic Church as the "Harlot of Rome," and how it had been responsible for the murder of "true Christians." His main church in Belfast was named *Martyrs' Memorial.* Inside the entryway of his church were the busts of many sixteen-century Protestants who were killed by Catholic Church leaders during the Reformation. Paisley not only charged that the Catholic Church was not Christian, he went on to say the Pope was the "anti-Christ" whose main task was to oppose true Christians, especially Ulster Protestants.

I have taken several Catholics and moderate Protestants to Reverend Paisley's main church in Belfast. This is how I often spent my Sunday evenings. On one occasion I took an Irish Catholic nun (not in her habit) to hear Paisley. She was reluctant to go, and afterwards she was so shaken by what she had heard that she could not drive her car out of the parking lot. As I drove her home that evening, she repeated the phrase again and again, "I never thought it was that bad." Another time I took a middle-class, moderate Protestant woman to hear Paisley. Her point of view was identical to the nun's reaction. Both had been born and raised in the North, and both were shocked by Paisley's ability to wind-up his congregation with an anti-Catholic message.

Paisley was a master at describing in great detail what Catholics will face when they die. One evening he asked everyone to close their eyes and imagine how it would feel to have your whole body on fire as you spent an eternity in Hell. I kept my eyes open and turned around and watched his parishioners behind me as he described the sensation of Catholics burning all over forever. Some of them had what I would call *a thin-lipped smile on their face.* I think many of them actually enjoyed hearing what will happen to Catholics when they all go to Hell.

More than any other man, Paisley was responsible for providing a religious justification for violence. One day I heard him give an impromptu sermon to a group of about 10 or 12 Protestant paramilitaries along a street barricade. There was no need for a bullhorn – his voice carried a long way despite the sound of traffic. He predicted that "Catholics would all go to Hell." The implied message was that loyalist paramilitaries could help God by speeding up the process. A popular slogan on the street in the Protestant parts of Belfast was, "Kill 'em all, let God sort 'em out."

The former loyalist paramilitary leader, David Ervine (1953-2007) told me that Paisley inspired anti-Catholic attitudes among Protestant paramilitaries throughout the North. Ervine said that when things "got really hot," Paisley would walk away. He went back to his church and Ervine and others "did the dirty deed and went to jail."

Contrary to his public reputation as a difficult man to deal with, I found Paisley to be an exceptionally friendly person. I interviewed him three times. It surprised me that he wanted talk about anything and everything except religion and politics. He seemed almost embarrassed when I quoted him and asked him to explain why Catholics were "all going to Hell." He pointed out quickly that there was still time for them to repent and that they didn't *need* to go to Hell. He spoke about his own public pronouncements as though they came from someone else.

On one occasion I was left alone in his office when he went across the hall to take a private phone call. I had about 20 minutes to myself to get up and walk around. On one wall, Paisley had a picture of himself and the former Ameican conservative, and segregationist, Republican US Senator Jesse Helms of North Carolina, with the inscription, "To My Friend Ian, Keep Up the Good Work in Northern Ireland." Right next to that was his honorary doctorate certificate from Bob Jones University in Greenville, South Carolina. Despite the fact that Paisley had an unearned degree, he was usually introduced by his followers as "Dr. Paisley." He was a powerful speaker who could be heard a great distance.

The public image of Reverend Paisley in Northern Ireland was that of a stern figure that would not compromise on principles. He saw the battle for Ulster as an epic struggle between good and evil. According to him, people on the "other side" were not just wrong, they were "doing the work of the Devil."

On one occasion, he extended that charge to include the entire British government. Paisley branded the peace process sponsored by the British as a part of the Devil's conspiracy to undermine Ulster Protestantism. He attempted to prove it by combining biblical numerology with politics. He counted the number of words in a British government communique and concluded there were "666 words" in the document, which proved (in his judgment) that the whole idea had the "Mark of the Beast." To religious fundamentalists, that number was a warning that the British government was under the direct influence of Satan. Some Belfast newspaper men (probable secular thinkers) counted the words and came up with the number of 694, which called the original charge into question, but Paisley defended his earlier count.

Most Ulster Protestants doubted that the conflict could be explained literally as a clash between divine and demonic forces, but deep down they confessed that God had probably taken a side in the conflict. I asked scores of Protestants whether they believed Paisley's extreme charge that the Pope was the anti-Christ. Most said "no," but many added a moment later, "Who knows for sure?"

Some may have questioned whether Ian Paisley was really serious about his charge against the Pope, but it must be remembered that when Paisley was a member of the European Parliament, he shouted insults at Pope John Paul II, who was speaking, and finally Paisley had to be forcibly ejected from the chamber so the Pope could finish his address.

The anti-Christ views of Paisley were well-known, but I found that there was a *parity* between the two communities on which side allegedly bears the "Mark of the Beast." Both Catholics and Protestants have told me that the Devil controls the other side. They went on to say that God has made this clear through decoding the names of Protestant and Catholic leaders. There was proof!

When the letters of the alphabet are given numerical values (and increased by 6 after each letter) a cult-like code emerges that permits individual names to be translated into numbers that reveal a secret association with the Devil. I have watched people meticulously print out a code where A has the value of 6, B = 12, D = 24 and so on up to X equaling 144, Y = 150, and Z = 156. Then they carefully spelled out the names of well-known people in a vertical format to see if their names added up to the dreaded number of "666." Keep in mind, the following calculations were written by folks on both sides to prove that the "other side" was headed up by the Devil. One of my friends (with a sense of humor) suggested that they both might be correct in their calculations!

I	=	54		G	=	42
A	=	6		E	=	30
N	=	84		R	=	108
				R	=	108
				Y	=	150
P	=	96				
A	=	6				
I	=	54		A	=	6
S	=	114		D	=	24
L	=	72		A	=	6
E	=	30		M	=	78
Y	=	150		S	=	114
		666				666

I have never seen this numerical theory in print, and it is highly doubtful many people would know about it or give it much credence. The only versions I ever saw were written down on yellow tablet paper. I was surprised that neither side seemed to know that the folks across town had the same code, but it had yielded a very different result. I wondered whether either side knew that this was something like a cross-community activity? But as far as I know, there was no communication between them. When asked where this came from, the answer I got from both communities was that it "was God's language," that it was a way "that God could warn us."

There was one guy I knew who kept bringing it up every time he came into the pub. He carried the code with him written down on yellow paper and he was convinced that it was a sign from Heaven. He and his friends ran the code on several well-known people (on the other side) in Belfast, but only one person came up with the dreaded "666 total." That seemed to prove the point that "God was guiding his hand."

I always wondered if any of the "believers" from one religion ever took the risk and ran the test against someone they followed. I doubt it because it was pretty much a one-way street that assured them what they already suspected: that the Devil had taken up the side of their enemy.

Catholics I knew gleefully pointed out that the code revealed that Ian Paisley had the "Mark of the Beast" on his back and was doing the work of the Devil. The evidence, they said, was "overwhelming." Some contended that Paisley could be credited with starting the Troubles in the mid-1960s when he demanded that the police remove an Irish flag out of store window on the Falls Road. The result was the first major riot of the conflict. They contended that Paisley's effort to divide the people proved beyond a doubt that he represented the demonic forces in the North of Ireland.

Protestants, however, were just as certain that Gerry Adams and his leadership in the IRA were the "work of the Devil." They told me many times that there were no problems in the North during the 1960s. To my surprise, they said Catholics and Protestants were "getting along just fine" until the IRA formed a paramilitary army in 1969. Many regarded Adams as the "brains behind the IRA." The conclusion was that Adams was the "evil master-mind" that caused Catholics to take up arms against the legally-constituted unionist government. They seemed equally certain that Irish republicans were still "doing the work of the Devil."

So, is there any evidence that religious groups have been responsible for what has happened in Northern Ireland? The case can be made that history clearly demonstrated that the rise of sectarianism goes right back to both religious institutions where families and whole neighborhoods learned their religious/political views. Neither the Catholic or the Protestant clergy accept any responsibility for the conflict. They blame it all on the likes of Paisley and Adams, but churches have themselves have played a dominating role for hundreds of years. Religious leaders on both sides have preached a "sermon of division" that fanned the flames of sectarianism for a long time.

"But why?" you might ask, "would the churches promote sectarianism?" We should recognize right away that the religious institutions of Northern Ireland have become the clear beneficiaries of a divided society. For most people, being a member of a church gives them a strong cultural/political identity. Church membership is really tribal membership. It provides a protective psychological fortress for individuals who are threatened by the opposing forces of the other side, and it excuses a lot of divisive behavior in both communities.

When the issue of religion comes up with most working-class people, it is clear that it has little or nothing to do with theology. Many of them do not believe in God, and don't go to religious services, but they claim to be members of their religious tribe.

Historically, when religion and national identity were merged in the North and South, it placed more power in the hands of the churches. In some cases, church leaders in both locations have been more important than elected political leaders in deciding public policy. Clearly, the clergy on both sides benefited from a situation where folks are "trapped" psychologically within their religious identities.

Religious leaders on both sides deny any role in promoting sectarianism. They speak of the "pain" they feel as they offer prayers for peace, but one wonders how sincere their anguish is as they are interviewed by the media. It seems to come too easy for them to condemn the violence without taking some responsibility for why it has happened.

Sectarianism is not an accident in Northern Ireland nor was it caused by Ian Paisley or Gerry Adams. There were church leaders long before them on both sides who blended religion and politics into a factional "this I believe statement" that was systematically taught. Young people were socialized into a society of opposing sectarian tribes.

Church leaders gained greater political/psychological power as a result of the Troubles. When the conflict is discussed, the words "Catholic" and "Protestant" immediately come to mind. Most of the towns in the North have Protestant and Catholic neighborhoods. Even the children know that their allies are in one church, and the other church has their enemies. The socialization process begins in early childhood and continues throughout life.

In current times there are some church leaders who still want to keep the children out of integrated schools, and there are others who condemn "mixed marriages." If the sectarian division between Catholics and Protestant would suddenly end, the clergy in Northern Ireland would immediately be less important. Then, in a pluralistic, non-sectarian world, would anyone wonder which side God had chosen in a political conflict?

27. Making Peace

It may surprise an outsider, but talking about peace in Northern Ireland was not a popular subject. The so-called "Peace People" in Belfast were always regarded as being a bit "soft headed," and not plugged into reality. I recall an older Protestant woman who said, "The peacemakers don't do any harm, and they might do some good, but the gunmen don't pay any attention to them." I think she was unknowingly speaking for a majority of the people in the North during the long war when the two communities were pitted against each other on a daily basis.

Early in the conflict there was a time when there was some expectation that peace would be restored, but that promise was short-lived. Two women (a Catholic and a Protestant) actually won the Nobel Peace Prize in 1977 for launching a peace movement in Northern Ireland the previous year. But the cross-community effort failed when it was opposed by paramilitaries on both sides. After a while, most people settled down in what appeared to be a war without end.

Despite the widespread pessimism in Belfast, I met several times with Mairead Corrigan Maguire, the Catholic recipient of the Nobel Prize. She was still working feverishly for peace, but most people saw her as "yesterday's person." I asked her if the prospects for peace had improved as a result of her work. She couldn't point to any recent successes, but she never gave up. Mairead, and people like her, were always willing to meet with anyone to talk about peace. There were several pockets of people like Mairead in Ulster, but no one seemed to take them very seriously.

When the issue of peace came up, most of the people I knew on both sides would shrug their shoulders and say, "I don't think we'll ever see the end of the conflict in my lifetime." Nearly everyone would nod their heads with a resigned look of helplessness. To make matters worse, some folks I knew thought peacemaking could be dangerous because it might mean the *other side* had won. This was especially true with Protestants who couldn't imagine a situation where both sides were satisfied.

At this point it might be well to put the peace process into a historical perspective. Up until the late 1960s, the so-called "Irish problem" was on the back burner in London. But after violence broke out in Northern Ireland in 1968-69, there was a need to send in the British army. Soon, British soldiers were all over the North. There was always a continuing discussion about how much this was costing the British taxpayer, but I didn't have any reliable personal information of what London had in mind until I met a British civil servant who had a very interesting story to tell.

My introduction to hearing about the modern British approach to the "Irish Problem" came about purely by accident. I was at a meeting of Protestant loyalists in a dingy meeting room in East Belfast and I heard an English accent from across the room. I was introduced to a guy named "Nick" who stood out because he was the only man in the room with a suit and a tie. I never knew his last name. We shook hands and talked briefly. Weeks later, I saw him again in the lobby of the Stormont Hotel in East Belfast. He remembered me and we went into the hotel bar and settled in for a long talk.

I think he was drawn to me first of all because I was not Irish. His first comment was demeaning to the whole Irish nation. In a low tone he declared, "At least the two of us are not like them." In a dramatic wave of his hand, he belittled the northern Irish on both sides. It was clear that he looked down on nearly everyone in Ulster. He kept talking about how the "paddies here were engaged in an endless war," and how the British were going to "save them from each other."

Nick and I sat in a corner and talked intently for at least two hours. I was full of questions. I asked why London hadn't taken a stronger stand with the loyalists. From my vantage point, the loyalists were able to frustrate the British at every turn. Why didn't the British lay down the law? Also, why did the officials in London continue to tolerate Protestant leaders like Ian Paisley, who Nick said was a was "an incurable bigot." I had so many unanswered questions.

While I was going through my litany of questions, Nick was making dramatic gestures and was raising his voice, "Let me tell you... let me tell you!" Nick was shouting and drawing the attention of others in the barroom. He eventually calmed down and rattled off the answers to my questions. He had an interesting story to tell.

First, he said, the Brits had to stay in Northern Ireland because they were afraid of what the loyalists would do if the army went back home. Nick narrowed his eyes as he looked at me and said, "We're here to keep the lid on. If we left, all hell would break loose."

Next, Nick responded to another of my questions when he said that the British Conservative Party had a special problem with Ulster politicians in the House of Commons. There were only a handful of Ulster Unionists in the Parliament, but the prime minister needed them on a close vote. Nick said the Ulster unionists were always threatening to create a political crisis. He went on to say, "We need those bastards in the Commons and they know it." As Nick spoke, he became more enraged because he had to acknowledge that Ulster Protestants had the British over a barrel on at least this one point.

Then Nick went on to tell me of his position in the British civil service. "My job," he said, "is to work with others to design political policies that will change political behavior in the North, despite what loyalists may do. He then rattled off all the recent examples of British efforts to bring the Dublin government into the process so they could slowly demonstrate that the North and South were going to be "merged at some levels." He stood up from his chair and said "We don't give a toss which flag flies over Belfast City Hall." We've been trying to get rid of these 'Belfast Bigots' for years, and now I think we've finally found a way."

Before I go on describing the conversation with Nick, it is important to note that our conversation was during the early 1990s, long before there was a serious chance for peace. Nick told me that the British were slowly grooming the Ulster preacher and politician Ian Paisley to take a more active role in the peace-making process. Nick said I would be surprised to know how egotistical and self-centered Paisley was. He said "the Belfast preacher" had an inflated idea of his own importance and that the British were feeding his ego by promising that they would place him in a key position if he would share power with Catholic nationalists. He added, "until we are ready, Paisley will continue to behave as he always has. But that will change soon."

That was several years ahead of the time when Nick's predictions began to come true.

My new British friend was describing a situation that would take place later in 2007 when Ian Paisley became the First Minister of the Northern Ireland government, serving with Martin McGuinness, Deputy First Minister (who was widely assumed to be the Chief of Staff of the Irish Republican

Army). It was a combination that no one thought possible, including me.

According to Nick, this "was in the cards" years before. He said there was a good chance that it would happen as planned. I had to disagree. I couldn't see how these two arch enemies could ever share power. I knew Paisley had spent his entire life condemning Catholics and the Pope, who he said was the anti-Christ.

Later, even when Paisley became the First Minister, he hung on to his declared position that he would never shake hands with a Catholic, but folks wondered how important that pledge was after he "went to bed with the Chief of the IRA." A lot of people, including myself, wondered how sincere Ian Paisley had been in his earlier pronouncements. He had made his whole career out of his anti-Catholic preaching. How could he ever change?

I had a special interest in Ian Paisley. Over a period of 61 years, he developed his anti-Catholic beliefs into a well-defined doctrine. It was his main theological message. Paisley seemed to enjoy talking about the Pope as the "worst sinner of all." When Pope John Paul II died in 2005, Ian Paisley declared in a conclusive statement, "This Romish man of sin is now in Hell."

The British must have thought they had a nearly impossible task when they talked Paisley into becoming the First Minister of the power-sharing government. He had built a career out of opposing *any* cooperation with Catholics. At an outside rally in front of Belfast City Hall, I remember hearing him shout, "NEVER, NEVER, NEVER." There were pictures all over East Belfast of the Reverend Ian Paisley with one word printed boldly, "No."

I remember seeing a huge banner wrapped around the dome of city hall stating, "Belfast Says No." This was the main message from Ian Paisley and Ulster Protestants for as long as anyone could remember. It was shocking to members of his religious flock when Ian Paisley announced that he was ready to share power with folks who, he had said, were being led by the anti-Christ.

Members of his church told me that they had followed him for more than 50 years, only to discover that he reversed his theological position on his most important pronouncement by going into a power-sharing government with Catholics. He had preached that "God was making a stand in Ulster against the Roman Catholic Church." Now he had turned his back on his own religious doctrine and joined in with Catholics to govern the North.

The result was that some of his outspoken parishioners opposed him publicly and forced him out as moderator of the Free Presbyterian Church. He was no longer able to preach in the church he had built. A lot of people, including me, wondered how this whole escapade could happen. This had to be the most notable political/religious flip-flop in northern Irish history.

Later, when Paisley and McGuinness became the new "odd couple of Northern Ireland," I went out looking for Nick in East Belfast so I could buy him a pint and congratulate him on his earlier predictions. I never saw him again. One of my sources told me Nick went back to London.

But in retrospect I should have taken his prediction more seriously. The British had been trying to get out of Northern Ireland for a long time. As early as 1972, the British secretly flew Gerry Adams and Martin McGinness to London for secret talks. That effort failed, but there were many attempts after that by the British to get the two sides together into some sort of workable power-sharing scheme.

According to Nick, the Brits had decided early on that they had to neutralize the *"main zealot"* in Northern Ireland before they could bring folks together in a power-sharing system. Their master strategy was to partially muzzle Ian Paisley when they made him First Minister of the power-sharing government. When he became First Minister, he was effectively silenced as the main critic of power sharing.

The British must have appealed to Paisley's sense of personal power. This was an opportunity for him to be in charge of process he had opposed all his professional life. But now, the big man (6-foot four inches, 240 pounds) with a booming voice could finally justify the idea of power-sharing with the enemy because he thought he could shape the policies to be decided.

I don't know if he realized that the whole concept of power-sharing would be the procedure that Catholic nationalists would use later to achieve equality in the North. Paisley assumed the position of First Minister on May 8, 2007 and resigned his office 13 months later on June 5, 2008 due to poor health. He died in 2014.

One could argue that his insistence of forever excluding Irish nationalists from the government died with him. He may not have recognized before his death that his apparent hunger for personal power made it possible for Irish nationalists to begin their drive to gain political power in the North of Ireland. So often in life, *extremely ambitious people frustrate their own efforts by their own hand.*

In some respects, this move rounded out Paisley's entire career as a religious/political leader. He had an important role in starting the sectarian riots in the 1960s with his insistence on removing an Irish flag from a store window on the Falls Road, and he was instrumental in ending the conflict by becoming the First Minister in 2007. I wonder if he ever looked at himself in the mirror while considering his personal involvement in events that both began and ended the conflict.

Since my meeting with Nick, the peace process has been on a rollercoaster with cease-fires, decommissioning of weapons, release of prisoners, all-night negotiations, deadlocks, and a flurry of diplomatic activities involving London, Dublin and Washington, D.C. The efforts to build peace have progressed at an unsteady and slow pace. Yet there are no signs that the British are giving up on their efforts to find some means of promoting non-violent politics in Northern Ireland.

In recent years, the good news is that the shooting war has seemingly ended. The Belfast Agreement (often called the Good Friday Agreement) was signed in 1998. There has been considerable back-sliding since then, but most of the guns are now silent. The bad news is that the ordinary people are now entering the most difficult phase of the process: dealing with their personal losses and getting on with their lives. Living in the aftermath of war is not as easy as it would seem. Many did not foresee that they would again relive those terrible portions of their past.

For reconciliation to occur, there is a need for a folks to sort out and clarify the events that caused them so much pain. There are so many questions that still need to be answered. People want to know who ordered the death of a loved one. Why was the investigation of the bombing of a particular pub not revealed to the public? Which paramilitary leader gave the word to assassinate a Belfast attorney at home on a Sunday afternoon in front of his family? Why were there no police around at the time? Are there people out there who are guilty of murder? Why was a particular event covered up by the government? Was the government involved in organizing a murder campaign?

This is the time when old newspaper clippings are read again to challenge the official reasons why a life was taken or why a child's death was considered to be just collateral damage. It has become a time when investigations are revealing that unarmed people were killed on both sides. To make matters worse, some of the culprits who planned the killings are still walking the streets today. Should they be charged? Will punishments of the guilty bring healing, or will it be just a matter of seeking revenge?

Then there are those who say it's time to put the past behind us. It will do no good to relive the past and increase the bitterness that occurs from digging up old issues. Some say that Ulster should turn the page and focus on a future where all these old painful animosities are put aside. But then comes the expected point of view that, "You can't sweep the dirty secrets of nearly 40 years of war under the rug."

Despite the public focus on "what happened," the British government has approved a measure in the House of Commons that would limit, or even shut down, "criminal investigations, legal proceedings, inquests, and police complaints" concerning the Northern Ireland conflict. The bill was opposed by all the political parties in Ireland (North and South). It was passed in the House of Commons and it was implemented in 2023.

So, the process of "putting the war behind us" is now supported by the British effort to "close it down." There are loud voices on both sides. Some want to unearth all the terrible things from the past, others want to bury nearly 40 years of accountability for the war. The shooting has stopped, but the debate goes on.

Perhaps the people on both sides should be realistic and recognize that *the graveyard will be the place where real political change will take place.* The "shouting war" won't end until some of the vengeful leaders pass from the scene. There's an old Irish saying that, "Some men improve the world by leaving it." That precept may be true in this case.

Maybe that's when the ordinary folks of Ulster will finally get around to forgiving their neighbors. Then, and only then, will the old grudges die with the past generation. Then, and only then, will a new generation finally turn the last page of the Northern Ireland peace process.

28. New Times with Old Questions

Today, looking down from a tall building, Belfast looks so peaceful. The red brick houses are all lined up in neat rows. Smoke from coal fires curl up in a predictable pattern. The winding streets appear so quaint and serene. Down below buses are running on time. People are moving in and out of professional offices, stores, and pubs. The current phrase of the chamber of commerce is: "Belfast is open for Business." Nearly everything looks better than it did 20 years ago, but appearances are deceptive. This city has been a troublesome place for well over 150 years.

There are many reasons why there has been so much turmoil here. The root causes (in no particular order) are political, historical, economic, religious, cultural, territorial, colonial, sectarian, and nationalistic. There have also been countless cases of police brutality, organized murders, assassinations, discrimination, and gerrymandering. Widespread sporadic riots between Protestants and Catholics have occurred here for as long as anyone can remember.

In recent years, the guns have been put aside, but one can still feel a division lurking in this land. Nearly everyone will tell you that they are happy the fighting has stopped, but they will also tell you that: *the absence of war is not peace.* There's an almost indescribable factor here that is not found in other parts of the world. It still hangs in the air. Do the underlying causes for a sectarian conflict ever go away completely?

So, what is it that hinders a real peace in Northern Ireland? I've thought about this during most of my adult life and I think it can be boiled down to a simple question that won't surprise anyone in the North. The enduring question is: "Are you British or Irish?" You might think they already know who they are. If you visit Northern Ireland, you will still come away with the conclusion that they appear to be absolutely certain of who they are! There are nationalistic flags, wall murals, and ethnic banners everywhere. But like other people around the world in communal conflicts, they *only find the need to proclaim their identity because they feel so insecure about their own status.*

When people feel no threat to their national identity, they no longer feel the need to shout it from the rooftops. But my northern Irish friends have never felt psychologically secure about their future – and because of this – they are obsessed with reminding themselves (and everyone else) that they are either British or Irish.

Especially in working-class neighborhoods, there is no middle ground! This preoccupation of nationalistic identity is tied to an underlying fear – true or not – that the other side wants to wipe them out as a people, and each has plenty of evidence that the threat has been real. When either side thinks of recent history, it is linked to an enflamed memory of "what they did to us," and each community is now united by a deep commitment to never let it happen again.

For Irish Catholics, it is a remembrance of massive discrimination against them while they were living in *their own country*. On the British Protestant side, they can't forget that they were faced with a rebellious threat to law and order while they were living in *their own country*.

Both sides are locked into a set of biased images they can't get out of their heads. Young people are still getting a dose of sectarian stories. As bad as the Troubles were, the mythological memories are even more long lasting. There is a "ghost" that lurks inside the Catholic and Protestant psyches that won't go away. People in both communities still have a feeling that they "are not whole." You might ask "Why is that important?"

A personal example will make my point. I remember years ago, when I was a teenager, I broke my leg in an accident. During the healing process I was completely preoccupied with my broken limb. Every inconvenience reminded me that I was not free to move about, that I was *not whole,* that I was not able to do the things I wanted to do. I didn't want to hear any comments about why I should adjust to my condition. My parents treated me well and even gave me special care, but I was focused only on my temporary physical misfortune. I could think of nothing else. It was only after the cast was taken off that I started to feel I was *whole* again – that I began to think about other daily challenges in life.

It may sound strange, but as a look back, I realized that taking off the cast on my leg *transformed me into feeling normal.* I forgot about my earlier preoccupation of "not feeling whole." I no longer even thought about my leg. Strangely, its importance to me diminished when it no longer held me back.

In some ways, that is the condition of Northern Ireland today. Everyone feels in their bones that the situation here is still not *normal*. It still has that nagging feeling of not being whole. *That other flag is still there.* Even though there is a new prosperity across the land, and new buildings are going up all over the city, some still feel unfulfilled because their country is still divided. Many sense that the last pages of the struggle are yet to be written. Then, and only then, will the people of Ulster feel like other peoples of the world.

When a nation feels *whole*, there is no particular need to wave flags and paint the curb stones in their national colors, to march through neighborhoods where they are not wanted, and shout nationalistic slogans from the barricades. Other nations have many problems, but they do have a basic security of knowing that they are whole – that they are complete – that they have only one national flag.

As time goes on, that feeling of *wholeness* may increase in Ulster, but I have doubts. I have a vivid memory of hearing terrible things from both sides. Hopefully, these oaths to get revenge will recede. Perhaps the question of being "Irish" or "British" may not preoccupy them on a daily basis. But in the meantime, the neighborhood walls will remain. There will still be quarrels over which culture is supreme, and everyone will notice which flag is being displayed on public buildings.

But there is yet another factor that plagues both sides in Northern Ireland. Neither of them can let go of their history. Both of them replay an emotionally-charged account of what happened to them in generations past. There is a lack of resolution in their memories – they can't get their historical obsessions out of their minds. The past hangs in the air like dark clouds over both sides of town. No amount of talk about the cease-fire, power-sharing, and the new prosperity will erase the feelings that they have been *wronged*, and that these transgressions have not yet been put right.

Irish Catholics are known around the world for not letting go of their history. There are tragic recollections exposed whenever they collectively "remember" the English invasion of Ireland, the loss of their land, the Famine, and the poverty that forced its people to leave a land that was owned by "outsider landlords." Terrible but true stories of the past have piled up in the Irish psyche and they cannot be put aside. It is not just the historians who "remember," it is the ordinary people as well. The Irish have been *damaged* at a deep level, and they have trouble putting that set of grievances behind them. They still feel the pain from British colonial policy that plagued them for hundreds of years. It is though a part of their national memory has been "broken," and it cannot be fixed.

Ulster Protestants are also caught up in a history they cannot leave behind. They came to make a permanent home in Ireland, but they found it to be an unfriendly land. Their families felt surrounded by Irish Catholics that never recognized the "British settler's right" to be in Ireland; they constantly felt the need to be on the alert. An attack could come at any time. Protestants in Ireland always sought the protection from their *mother country,* who promised to support them, but even in the early years, the settlers felt a separation from their home base across the water. They had a constant fear about being left behind. In recent years that threat of being abandoned has grown. Irish Protestants are haunted by a history of being loyal to their British heritage, but they feel that folks in mainland Britain are no longer loyal to them.

But there's another fact of life that complicates this quest of the Ulster people on both sides. It is that the rest of the world no longer cares about them anymore. There is no wide-spread appreciation for their sense of loss. The guns are silent now, so outsiders say, "Get over it, it's time to move on." But many northern Irish can't "get over it." It's a part of who they are.

In the case of Northern Ireland, these two peoples are in transition to *a place that is new to them.* It is not a matter of *restoring* the peace – in 800 years, they have never known a real peace. The earliest pages of their combined history were etched with the byproducts of political, cultural, and religious conflict. Terrible things were done in the name of building a colony in Ireland. At best, it will be difficult for these people on both sides to learn the art of living in a real democratic society based on equality. It should be remembered that what is commonplace in other parts of the world, is a *new idea* in Northern Ireland. It is being tried here for the first time.

Getting them to stop the shooting war took most of the twentieth century, but it *may* have been finally achieved. Getting them to trust each other and share political power is the challenge of the twenty-first century. Who knows how long that will take? Time moves at a different pace in Ulster.

It is said that a few years ago, a modern passenger plane was landing at Belfast's international airport. The pilot came on the intercom and announced, "We are landing in Northern Ireland – set your clocks back three hundred years." People from outside of Ireland laughed at the story, but the northern Irish on both sides, didn't think it was funny because it's was too close to being true.

About the Author

Bill Meulemans is an American political science professor who has spent most of his time listening to folks that were doing the fighting and dying in Northern Ireland and Israel.

Early in his career, he was appointed to a position as a Professor of Political Science at Southern Oregon College (now Southern Oregon University) where he brought extremist group members of the far left and right into his classroom. Later, he did a series of interviews with members of the Ku Klux Klan in several southern states. After a long tenure at Southern Oregon University, Meulemans was awarded a Fulbright Scholarship to Israel where he followed his regular approach to politics: he spent his days with the Israeli government in Jerusalem and his evenings with the Palestinians in Ramallah.

After one year, he accepted a teaching post as a Professor of Politics at The Queen's University of Belfast, where he was to remain on the teaching faculty for 11 years. Belfast became his home away from home – he lived and worked in both Catholic and Protestant neighborhoods. After his time in Ireland, he returned to the United States as a Professor of Political Science at Portland State University where he offered a course titled, "War and Peace in

Northern Ireland."

In addition to his university work, Meulemans worked as a staff aide in the US House of Representatives for the Committee on Education and Labor. He has written several books and served on many boards and commissions in the United States and Northern Ireland. In a secondary role, he was a newspaper reporter, a radio and television political commentator, and he also served as a political organizer for opposing racial groups, law enforcement agencies, business professionals, communities in conflict, and tribes of American Indians in southwestern Oregon.

An Invitation to Write a Book Review

To My Readers,

Thank you for reading my book. I am always interested in hearing your feedback.

You can lead other readers from around the country to discover this book.

While the book is still fresh in your mind, why not write a book review on *Amazon, Apple, Kobo, Barnes and Noble* or wherever you purchased the book.

You can google *Amazon* or the other vendors with the book title to reach the book review location.

Your short review of this book may influence others who are interested in the subject.

You may also review any of my current books:

Belfast: Both Sides Now. (2013)

How the Left and Right Think. (2019)

Dynamiting the Siskiyou Pass. (2023)

Belfast Flashbacks. (2024)

You are also welcome to visit my website: **billmeulemans.com**

Thank you,
Bill Meulemans